PHONETIC DRILL READER

Phonetic Drill Reader

J. D. O'Connor

Reader in Phonetics in the
University of London

Cambridge University Press

Cambridge

London · New York · Melbourne

Published by the Syndics of the Cambridge University Press
The Pitt Building, Trumpington Street, Cambridge CB2 1RP
Bentley House, 200 Euston Road, London NW1 2DB
32 East 57th Street, New York, NY 10022, USA
296 Beaconsfield Parade, Middle Park, Melbourne 3206, Australia

ISBN 0 521 08582 9

First published 1973
Reprinted 1976 1977

Printed in Great Britain at the
University Press, Cambridge

Contents

Introduction

This book has been written to provide practice material for foreign students of English who want to work systematically at improving their English pronunciation. Each of the twenty-five pieces in it is a dialogue in a colloquial style and, it is hoped, with a certain degree of naturalness; but each contains a high concentration of examples for the drilling of particular features of pronunciation. The book is designed to accompany my *Better English Pronunciation (BEP)* and the order of presentation in this book reflects the order there. I have given page references to *Better English Pronunciation*, and I would recommend the student to have another look at the relevant pages in it before starting on each piece, and perhaps to go over the practice material there. Intonation is marked throughout in the simplified way explained in Chapter 7 of *Better English Pronunciation*.

Each piece should be studied carefully and repeatedly; it may help if you underline particular difficulties. Aim at accuracy and smoothness – speed is not essential and can be harmful in the early stages.

University College London   J. D. O'CONNOR

ig'zɑːmp|z　　'fin　　'θin　　'væt　　'ðæt
　　　　　　　ˌɔfə　　ˌɔːθə　　'lʌvə　　'brʌðə
　　　　　　　'def　　'deθ　　'klouv　　'klouð

i'lizəbəθ ən 'deivid

i'lizəbəθ　ai hæd ə 'foun kɔːl frəm 'mʌðə ðis ˌiːvniŋ‖
'deivid　'hau 'ɑː ðei ˌbouθ‖
i'lizəbəθ　'ou| ðɛə 'bouθ əz 'fit əz 'fliːz‖
'deivid　its 'fʌni| aiv biːn 'θiŋkiŋ‖ 'wai nɔt in'vait jɔː 'mʌðər ən ˌfɑːðə|
　　　tə 'træv| 'ʌp tə 'pəːθ wið əs| wen wiː 'vizit 'ɑːθə ˌðɛə‖
i'lizəbəθ　ðæts 'veri 'θɔːtf| ɔv juː‖ ai 'θiŋk ðeid 'lʌv tə ˌhæv ði: ˌinviˌteiʃn|
　　　bət ai 'rɑːðə ˇdaut| weðər 'aiðər əv ðəm wud 'fiːl 'breiv iˌnʌf‖ 'fænsi
　　　ðæt 'θauzn̩d mail 'dʒəːni| in ə 'nɔt veri 'kʌmftəb| ˌkɑː| wið ðə 'θriː
　　　'tʃildrən‖ ai 'bliːv ðeid 'vjuː ðə 'houl ˇθiŋ| 'rɑːðər ʌn'feivrəbli‖ ən
　　　'dount fəˇget| ðət 'θiːou wil bi 'tiːðiŋ bai ˌðen‖
'deivid　ðɛə 'fɛəli 'tʌf ðou ˌlʌv‖ 'θiŋk əv 'ðæt 'taim ðə 'faiv əv əs 'went
　　　ɔf tə 'fælməθ təˌgeðə‖ ðə 'weðə wəz 'fraitf| ðə 'fuːd wəz 'vail| ənd
　　　'ɑːðə gɔt dif'θiəriə‖ bət 'ðei ˌθɔːt| ðət 'evriθiŋ wəz 'lʌvli‖
i'lizəbəθ　ˌˇðæts ə 'fæmli 'miθ‖ it wəz 'nevə difˌθiəriə‖ ðə 'truːθ ˇiz| ðət
　　　it wəz 'nʌθiŋ ˇʌðə| ðən ə 'nɔt veri si'viə 'fiːvə hiː ˌgɔt| ɑːftə 'beiðiŋ
　　　in ðə 'rivə ˌðɛə‖ wiðin 'θriː ˇdeiz| hiː wəz 'fitə ðən 'evə‖
'deivid　jɔː 'mʌðə ˌstil ˌθiŋks əv it əzˈdifˌθiəriə‖ hau'evə| 'miθ ɔː 'nou
　　　miθ| ðei 'bouθ 'θʌrəli 'revd in it‖
i'lizəbəθ　bət 'ðæt wəz 'naintiːn 'fifti 'faiv‖ ðei wə 'fiftiːn 'jəːz 'jʌŋgə
　　　ˌðen‖ ðɛə 'bouθ 'ouvə 'sevn̩ti ˌnau| ənd ai 'θiŋk ðeid 'faind it
　　　'difək|t tə səˌvaiv ðæt ˌsɔːt əv ˌθiŋ ˌðiːz ·deiz‖ ðei 'hæf tə luk 'ɑːftə
　　　ðəmˌselvz| 'fɛəli 'kɛəfəli‖
'deivid　ai 'gæðə juː 'dount 'feivər in'vaitiŋ ðəm ˌðen‖
i'lizəbəθ　juː 'gæðə 'rait mai ˌlʌv| 'seiv jɔː 'breθ‖ aiv 'faund ouvə ðə 'lɑːst
　　　'θriː ɔː 'fɔː ˇjəːz| ðət its 'fɑː ˇseifə| tə let 'sliːpiŋ 'mʌðəz ən 'fɑːðəz
　　　'lai‖

Examples   fin   thin   vat   that
offer   author   lover   brother
deaf   death   clove   clothe

Elizabeth and David

Elizabeth   I had a phone call from Mother this evening.

David   How are they both?

Elizabeth   Oh, they're both as fit as fleas.

David   It's funny, I've been thinking; why not invite your mother and father to travel up to Perth with us when we visit Arthur there?

Elizabeth   That's very thoughtful of you. I think they'd love to have the invitation, but I rather doubt whether either of them would feel brave enough. Fancy that thousand-mile journey in a not very comfortable car with the three children. I believe they'd view the whole thing rather unfavourably. And don't forget that Theo will be teething by then.

David   They're fairly tough, though, love. Think of that time the five of us went off to Falmouth together. The weather was frightful, the food was vile, and Arthur got diphtheria. But they thought that everything was lovely.

Elizabeth   That's a family myth, it was never diphtheria. The truth is that it was nothing other than a not very severe fever he got after bathing in the river there. Within three days he was fitter than ever.

David   Your mother still thinks of it as diphtheria. However, myth or no myth, they both thoroughly revelled in it.

Elizabeth   But that was 1955, they were fifteen years younger then. They're both over seventy now, and I think they'd find it difficult to survive that sort of thing these days. They have to look after themselves fairly carefully.

David   I gather you don't favour inviting them, then.

Elizabeth   You gather right, my love, save your breath. I've found over the last three or four years that it's far safer to let sleeping mothers and fathers lie.

ig'zɑːmp|z 'θin ˋðen 'suː 'zuː 'θik ˋsik ˋðen 'zen
         'riːθ 'riːð 'luːs 'luːz 'pɑːθ 'pɑːs 'briːð 'briːz

'eθ| ən ˋsæm

ˋeθ| 'ðis 'stjuːpid ˇsiŋks| 'nʌθiŋ bət ə 'filθi 'njuːsn̩s||
ˋsæm ,ziŋk|| ˋwɔt ,ziŋk||
ˋeθ| ˋsiŋk juː ,bliðəriŋ ,æs| ˋsiŋk|| ðis ,stjuːpid| ,mesi| ,sliːzi| 'θʌrəli
    'louðsəm ˇθiŋ| ðət 'kɔːlz itself ə 'kitʃən ˋsiŋk|| aiv siːn 'naisə 'siŋks
    ðən ˇðis| 'θroun in ðə ˋdʌsbin|| ail 'smæʃ it tə 'piːsiz ,wʌn ə ðiːz ·deiz||
ˋsæm ai 'hɑːdli 'θiŋk its 'nesəsri tə 'gou tə ˋðouz ,leŋθs|| ˋwɔt ɔn 'əːθs
    ˋbɔðəriŋ juː||
ˋeθ| aim 'sik tə 'deθ əv it| ən ,ðæts ðə 'sɔləm ˇtruːθ|| ðə 'sɔːt əv 'siŋks
    ðɛə 'juːziŋ in 'hauziz ˇnauədeiz| ə 'steinləs ˋstiːl| ɔː 'ziŋk| ɔː 'sʌmθiŋ
    əv ˋðæt ,sɔːt||
ˋsæm ə 'ziŋk ˋsiŋk|| it hæz 'rɑːðər ə 'nais ˇsaund| bət ai 'dount θiŋk ai
    ˇfænsi ə ,ziŋk ,siŋk ·sʌmhau|| 'nɔː 'steinləs ˋstiːl| ˋaiðə|| 'bouθ
    ik'sesivli ˋnɔizi ai ʃud ,θiŋk|| ˋeni,wei| ai 'θɔːt 'ðæt wəz ðə 'siŋk juː
    'speʃli ˋtʃouz| wen 'mistə 'smiθ wəz di'zainiŋ ðə ,haus||
ˋeθ| its 'θəːti 'θri: ˋjəːz sins ,mistə ,smiθ ,fəːs di,zaind ,ðis ,haus||
ˋsæm 'θəːti 'θri: ˋjəːz|| ˋðæt 'meiks it 'naintiːn θəːti 'siks|| ˋjes| it wəz
    in ðə 'sʌmər əv 'θəːti 'siks ðət wiː wə ˋmærid| ˋwɔzn̩t it|| sou jɔː
    'neks ˇbəːθdiz| jɔː 'fifti ˋsiksθ||
ˋeθ| ˋjes| ənd 'jɔːz | biː jɔː ˋsikstiəθ|| juː 'stil siːm 'riːznəbli ˋhelθi ,ðou||
ˋsæm ˇθæŋks|| ai 'mʌs ˋsei| ai 'dount fiːl 'eniθiŋ laik ˇsiksti|| bət ˋðen|
    its im'pɔsəb| tə ˇriəlaiz| ðət 'jɔːr ɔːlmoust 'fifti ˋsiks||
ˋeθ| ˇθæŋk juː ,switi||
ˋsæm 'bai ðə ˋwei| 'wenz auə 'θəːti 'θəːd ˋwediŋ æni,vəːsri ðen||
ˋeθ| juː 'ɔːlwiz fə,get ,ðæt deit|| nau 'θiŋk||
ˋsæm 'lets ˋsiː|| ðə 'siks'tiːnθ əv ,dʒuːn||
ˋeθ| ðə ˋsevn̩tiːnθ||
ˋsæm 'ɑː ˋjes| ðə ˋsevn̩tiːnθ|| 'dʒuːn ðə 'sevn̩ˋtiːnθ|| bət 'ðæts təˋdei||
ˋeθ| 'keim ðə ˋdɔːn|| 'æt ˋlɑːst||
ˋsæm ai ˋsiː|| it wəz ˋmiː juː wə ,krɔs wið| ,rɑːðə ðən ðə ,siŋk||
ˋeθ| əf ˋkɔːs it ,wɔz juː ,sili ,θiŋ||

Examples thin   then   Sue   zoo   thick sick   then   Zen
          wreath   wreathe   loose lose   path   pass   breathe breeze

Ethel and Sam

Ethel This stupid sink's nothing but a filthy nuisance!

Sam Zinc? What zinc?

Ethel Sink, you blithering ass, sink. This stupid, messy, sleazy, thoroughly loathesome thing that calls itself a kitchen sink. I've seen
nicer sinks than this thrown in the dustbin. I'll smash it to pieces one
of these days.

Sam I hardly think it's necessary to go to those lengths. What on earth's
bothering you?

Ethel I'm sick to death of it and that's the solemn truth. The sort of
sinks they're using in houses nowadays are stainless steel or zinc or
something of that sort.

Sam A zinc sink. It has rather a nice sound, but I don't think I fancy a
zinc sink somehow; nor stainless steel, either; both excessively noisy,
I should think. Anyway, I thought that was the sink you specially
chose when Mr Smith was designing the house.

Ethel It's thirty-three years since Mr Smith first designed this house.

Sam Thirty-three years? That makes it 1936. Yes, it was in the summer
of '36 that we were married, wasn't it? So your next birthday's your
fifty-sixth.

Ethel Yes, and yours will be your sixtieth. You still seem reasonably
healthy, though.

Sam Thanks. I must say I don't feel anything like sixty. But then, it's
impossible to realise that you're almost fifty-six.

Ethel Thank you, sweetie.

Sam By the way, when's our thirty-third wedding anniversary, then?

Ethel You always forget that date. Now think.

Sam Let's see. The sixteenth of June?

Ethel The seventeenth.

Sam Ah, yes, the seventeenth. June the seventeenth? But that's today!

Ethel Came the dawn. At last.

Sam I see. It was me you were cross with rather than the sink.

Ethel Of course it was, you silly thing.

igˈzɑːmp|z   ˈsed   ˈzed   ˈʃed

                 ˈæs   ˈæz   ˈæʃ   ˈruːʒ

                 ˈluːsə   ˈluːzə   ˈpreʃə   ˈtreʒə

                         ˈsuːzi ən ˈʃɔːn

ˈʃɔːn   ai ˈmʌs ˌsei| ðət ˈʃɔpiŋ ɔn ˇtjuːzdiz| inˈsted əv ˇsætədiz| iz ə ˈpɔzətiv

ˈpleʒə‖ ˈsou mʌtʃ ˈles ˈkeiɔs ən kənˈfjuːʒŋ‖ ˈhæv wiː ˌfiniʃt‖

ˈsuːzi ˇɔːlmoust‖ ðɛəz ə ˈʃɔp in ˈkrouʒə ˌstriːt| ðət ˈstɔks ðə ˈsɔːt əv

ˈsænd|z ai ˌwɔnt‖

ˈʃɔːn   juː ˈdount ˈjuːʒ|i ˌget jɔː ˌʃuːz ˌðɛə| ˌduː juː‖

ˈsuːzi   ˌnou| bət ai ˈjuːz ðəm əˇkeiʒnəli| if mai ˈjuːʒuəl ˌʃɔp| ˈhæzŋt gɔt

ðə ˈrait ˈsaiziz| ən ˈʃeidz ən ˌsou ɔn‖

ˈʃɔːn   ˈiz ˌðis ðə ·ʃɔp| ɔn ði: ˈɔpəzit ˈsaid ə ðə ˌstriːt‖ ðɛəz ə ˇnoutis| ðət

sez preˈstiːʒ ˈʃuːz fə ˈleʒər ən ˈpleʒə‖

ˈsuːzi   ˈjes| ˈðis iz ˌit‖ ən ˈðouz ə ðə ˈsænd|z ai ˌwɔnt‖

ˈʃɔːn   ˈðouz ˌbeiʒ wʌnz‖ ˈveri ˈseksi‖ ðei ʃud ˈkɔːz ə senˈseiʃŋ| əˌmʌŋst

auə ˈsiəriəs ˇneibəz‖

ˈsuːzi   ai ˈʃudŋt bi ˈsɔri| tə ˈʃɔk ˈðouz ˌsoubə ˌsaidid ˌsitizŋz‖ ˈlets gou

inˈsaid| ən ˈsiː‖ (tuː əˈsistənt) ˈðouz ˈbeiʒ ˈsænd|z in ðə ˈwindou‖

ˈhæv juː ə ˈsaiz ˌsevŋ‖

əˈsistənt   aim ˈsou ˌsɔri‖ ˈðouz ə ˈsaiz ˈsiks| ən ðɛə ðə ˈlɑːs ˈpɛər əv

ˈsænd|z in ðə ˈʃɔp‖ wiː hæv ˈmæsiz əv ˈʌðə kaindz əv ˌkæʒuəl ˌʃuːz|

bət ˈsænd|z ə ˈfiniʃt fə ˌðis ·siːzŋ‖

ˈsuːzi   ai səˇpouz| æʒ ˇjuːʒuəl| aim ˈsʌfriŋ frəm ðis əbˈsəːd diˇluːʒŋ| ðət

ˈsʌmə ˌʃuːz| ər ˈin ðə ˈʃɔps in ˈsʌmə‖

ˈʃɔːn   it ˌsiːmz ə ˌriːznəb| kənˌkluːʒŋ‖

əˈsistənt   ˈou ˈnou sə‖ in ˇsʌmə| wi ə ˈbizi ˈseliŋ ˈʃuːz fər ˈɔːtəm‖

ˈʃɔːn   bət ˈʃuəli ˌsuːzi| ˈðis ˈizŋt ðə ˇfəːst əˌkeiʒŋ juːv ikˌspiəriənst

ˌðis‖ ˌiz it ‖

ˈsuːzi   its ˈhæpŋd ˈdʌzŋz əv ˌtaimz| bət ai ˈsimpli ˈkɑːnt riˈzist ˈmeikiŋ

ðə ˈseim miˈsteik ɔn ðə ˈnekst əˌkeiʒŋ| ənd aim ˈɔːlwiz səˌpraizd‖

ˈʃɔːn   ˈpræps ˈðæt ikˈspleinz ðə ˈsteit əv jɔː ˈʃuːz ət ˈprezŋt‖

əˈsistənt   ˈʃæl ai ˈʃou juː ˈsʌm əv ðiːz ˌkæʒuəlz ·mædəm‖

ˈsuːzi   ˈjes ˌpliːz‖ ˈlets ˈstɑːt wið ðouz ˈsweid ˈslipəz| wið ðə ˈzig zæg

dekəˈreiʃŋz ɔn ðə ˈsaidz‖

əˈsistənt   ə ˈpleʒə ˌmædəm‖

Examples   said   Zed   shed
                  ass   as   ash   rouge
                  looser loser pressure treasure

Suzie and Shaun

Shaun   I must say that shopping on Tuesdays instead of Saturdays is a positive pleasure, so much less chaos and confusion. Have we finished?

Suzie   Almost. There's a shop in Crozier Street that stocks the sort of sandals I want.

Shaun   You don't usually get your shoes there, do you?

Suzie   No, but I use them occasionally if my usual shop hasn't got the right sizes and shades and so on.

Shaun   Is this the shop on the opposite side of the street? There's a notice that says: '*Prestige* shoes for leisure and pleasure.'

Suzie   Yes, this is it. And those are the sandals I want.

Shaun   Those beige ones? Very sexy, they should cause a sensation amongst our serious neighbours.

Suzie   I shouldn't be sorry to shock those sober-sided citizens. Let's go inside and see. (*To assistant*) Those beige sandals in the window, have you a size seven?

Assistant   I'm so sorry, those are size six and they're the last pair of sandals in the shop. We have masses of other kinds of casual shoes, but sandals are finished for this season.

Suzie   I suppose, as usual, I'm suffering from this absurd delusion that summer shoes are in the shops in summer.

Shaun   It seems a reasonable conclusion.

Assistant   Oh no, sir. In summer we're busy selling shoes for autumn.

Shaun   But surely, Suzie, this isn't the first occasion you've experienced this, is it?

Suzie   It's happened dozens of times, but I simply can't resist making the same mistake on the next occasion. And I'm always surprised.

Shaun   Perhaps that explains the state of your shoes at present.

Assistant   Shall I show you some of these casuals, madam?

Suzie   Yes, please. Let's start with those suede slippers with the zig-zag decorations on the sides.

Assistant   A pleasure, madam.

igˈzɑːmp|z ˈtʃouk ˈdʒouk ˈruːʃ ˈruːʒ ˈʃin ˈtʃin ˈleʒə ˈledʒə
ˈritʃ ˈridʒ ˈouʃn̩ ˈklouʒə ˈwɔʃ ˈwɔtʃ ˈbeiʒ ˈpeidʒ

ˈdʒeni ən ˈʃɑːlət

ˈdʒeni ˈhæv juː ˈfiniʃt jɔː ˌʃɔpiŋ‖
ˈʃɑːlət ˈgreiʃəs ˌnou| aiv ˈdʒʌs ˈstɑːtid‖ ai ˈʃɑːnt bi ˈfiniʃt biˈfɔː ˈlʌnʃˌtaim‖
ˈdʒeni juː ˈjuːʒli ˈmænidʒ tə ˈʃɔp ɔn ˈfraidiz| ˌdountʃuː‖
ˈʃɑːlət ˈjes| bət ai ˈhæd tə ˈtʃeindʒ mai əˈproutʃ ˌðis wiːk‖ ˈdʒɔn wəz ˈindʒəd in ə ˈkɑː ˌkræʃ ˌjestədi| ən ðɛə wəz ˈsʌtʃ ə kəˇmouʃn̩| ðət aid ˈnou ˈtʃɑːns tə ˈʃɔp əˈtɔːl‖
ˈdʒeni ˈou| ˈʃɑːlət| mai ˈeindʒəl‖ ˈhau ˈretʃid‖ ˈiz ˈdʒɔn ˌbædli ·indʒəd‖
ˈʃɑːlət ˈnou| ˈdʒʌʃ ˈʃeikən ˌæktʃəli‖ ðə kəˈliʒŋ ˈrenʃt iʒ ˇʃouldər| ən iː hæd ə ˈtʌtʃ əv ˈʃɔk| bət ˈnʌθiŋ ˌmʌtʃ‖ bət ðə ˈtʃæp uː ˈkræʃt ˇintuː im| ˈwɔznt̩ sou ˈfɔːtʃənət‖ ˈhiː ˈfræktʃəd iz ˈskʌl‖ ˈænd iz ˈdʒɔː‖ əz ˈwel əz səm ˈsuːpəˈfiʃl ˌindʒəriz‖ ðei ˈrʌʃt im tə ðə ˈkæʒuəlti diˌpɑːtmənt| ənd iː ˈhæd ən iˈməːdʒənsi ɔpəˌreiʃn̩‖ ai ˈhæd ə ˈtʃæt tə ðə ˈsəːdʒən in ˈtʃɑːdʒ dʒʌs ˌnau| ənd ˈhiː ˌsed| hiː ʃud hæv ə ˈgudiʃ ˈtʃɑːns‖
ˈdʒeni ˈhau did ðə kəˈliʒŋ ˈhæpən‖
ˈʃɑːlət wel its ˈdifək|t tə ˈriːtʃ ə kəŋˈkluːʒŋ‖ ˈdʒɔnz ˇmaind| iz in ˈsʌm kənˈfjuːʒŋ| bət iːz ˈpriti ˈʃuə ðət iː wəz ˈsteiʃənəri| ət ˈðæt ˈdʒʌŋkʃŋ bai ðə ˈtʃəːtʃ‖
ˈdʒeni ˈwitʃ ˌtʃəːtʃ‖ sn̩t ˌdʒeimziz‖
ˈʃɑːlət ˈjes| ən ˈðis ˈretʃid ˈtʃæp in iz ˇdʒægjuːə| dʒʌs ˈtʃɑːdʒd intə ðə ˈbæk əv im‖
ˈdʒeni ˈʃeimfl̩‖ ˈiz ðɛə ˈmʌtʃ ˈdæmidʒ tə ˌjɔːz‖
ˈʃɑːlət ðə ˈgærɑːʒ ə ˈmeikiŋ ə prəˈviʒnl̩ inˌspekʃn̩| fər inˈʃuərəns ˌpəːpəsiz‖ ən wiː ˈʃɑːmp bi ˈʃuə til ðei ˈfiniʃ it‖ ðiː ˈendʒənz ʌnˈtʌtʃt| bət ðə səˇspenʃn̩| ən ðə ˈkoutʃˌwəːk| ə ˈdæmidʒd fə ˈʃuə‖
ˈdʒeni ˈgud ˈgreiʃəs‖
ˈʃɑːlət ən ðə pəˈliːs ˈhævn̩t ˈmeid ə diˈsiʒŋ ˌjet| ˈweðə tə ˈtʃɑːdʒ im wið ˈdeindʒərəs ˈdraiviŋ‖
ˈdʒeni ˈhuː| ˌdʒɔn‖
ˈʃɑːlət ˈnou ˈnou‖ bət ai ˈʃudn̩t ˈreliʃ əˈpiəriŋ biˈfɔːr ə ˇmædʒistreit| ˈmʌtʃ ˈles ə ˈdʒʌdʒ‖
ˈdʒeni ai ʃud ˈθiŋk ˈnɔt‖ ˈgiv ˌdʒɔn auə ˌbest ˌwiʃiz‖ ai ˈmʌs ˈdæʃ tə ðə ˈbutʃəz| biˈfɔːr iː ˈʃʌts fə ˈlʌnʃ‖

Examples	choke joke	ruche rouge	shin chin	leisure ledger
	rich ridge	ocean closure	wash watch	beige page

Jennie and Charlotte

Jennie   Have you finished your shopping?

Charlotte   Gracious, no. I've just started. I shan't be finished before lunch-time.

Jennie   You usually manage to shop on Fridays, don't you?

Charlotte   Yes, but I had to change my approach this week. John was injured in a car crash yesterday, and there was such a commotion that I'd no chance to shop at all.

Jennie   Oh, Charlotte, my angel! How wretched! Is John badly injured?

Charlotte   No, just shaken, actually. The collision wrenched his shoulder, and he had a touch of shock, but nothing much. But the chap who crashed into him wasn't so fortunate. He fractured his skull and his jaw, as well as some superficial injuries. They rushed him to the casualty department and he had an emergency operation. I had a chat to the surgeon in charge just now and he said he should have a goodish chance.

Jennie   How did the collision happen?

Charlotte   Well, it's difficult to reach a conclusion. John's mind is in some confusion, but he's pretty sure that he was stationary at that junction by the church.

Jennie   Which church? St James's?

Charlotte   Yes, and this wretched chap in his Jaguar just charged into the back of him.

Jennie   Shameful. Is there much damage to yours?

Charlotte   The garage are making a provisional inspection for insurance purposes, and we shan't be sure till they finish it. The engine's untouched, but the suspension and the coach-work are damaged for sure.

Jennie   Good gracious!

Charlotte   And the police haven't made a decision yet whether to charge him with dangerous driving.

Jennie   Who? John?

Charlotte   No, no. But I shouldn't relish appearing before a magistrate, much less a judge.

Jennie   I should think not. Give John our best wishes. I must dash to the butcher's before he shuts for lunch.

igˈzɑːmp|z   ˈjet   ˈdʒet   ˈjɔːz   ˈdʒɔːz
            ˈdjuːn   ˈdʒuːn   ˈindjə   ˈindʒə
            ˈjuːs   ˈdʒuːs   ˈlɔːjə   ˈdʒɔːdʒə

ˈhjuː ən ˈdʒɔːdʒ

ˈdʒɔːdʒ ˈdid juː ˈriːd ˈdʒɔn ˌjʌŋz ·peidʒ| in ˈtjuːzdiz ˌgɑːdjən| ɔn ˈjuərəˈpiən ˌstjuːdn̩ts‖

ˈhjuː ˈjes| ən it wəz ə ˈdʒɔli ˈjuːsf| ˈkɔntriˈbjuːʃn̩‖ ˈdʒɔn ˈjʌŋ ˈdʒenrəli ˈmeiks miː ˈfjuəriəs| ən ai riˈdʒekt iz ˈvjuːz iˈmiːdjətli| əz ə ˈhɔdʒ ˌpɔdʒ| əv ˈil daiˌdʒestid| ˈsjuːdou intəˈlektjuəl ˈgɑːbidʒ‖ bət ˈjestədiz ˌpeidʒ| wəz ˈdʒenjuinli ˈvæljuəb|| fər ə ˈtʃeindʒ‖ ai inˈdʒɔid it‖

ˈdʒɔːdʒ ˈstreindʒ ðət ˈjuː inˌdʒɔid it ˌhjuː‖ ʌnˈles jɔː ˈvjuːz ɔn ˈstjuːdn̩ts əv ˈtʃeindʒd‖ jɔː ˈnɔt ˈjuːʒ|i ˈveri ˈdʒenrəs in jɔː ˌdʒʌdʒmənts əv ˌjuːθ‖

ˈhjuː ˈnɔt ˌdʒenrəs‖ jɔː ˈdʒoukiŋ ˌdʒɔːdʒ‖ ˈai ˈdʒʌdʒ ˈstjuːdn̩ts| ˈænd ˈʌðə ˌjʌŋ ˌpiːp|| wið ˈdʒʌst əz ˈmʌtʃ dʒenəˌrɔsəti| əz ai ˈdʒʌdʒ hjuːˈmænəti in ˈdʒenrəl‖ ðɛəz ˈnou ikˈskjuːs fə ˈtʃeindʒiŋ wʌnz ˈvæljuːz| ˈdʒʌs bikɔz ðə ˈsʌbdʒikt iz əˈnʌðər ˈeidʒ ˌgruːp‖

ˈdʒɔːdʒ ˈjes‖ ˈdount iˈmædʒən aim diˈspærədʒiŋ jɔː ˈdʒʌdʒmənt ˌhjuː| ˈdʒʌs ˈtʃæləndʒiŋ jɔː ˈjuːs əv ðə ˈseim ˈjɑːdˌstik| fə ðə ˈjʌŋgə dʒenəˌreiʃn̩| ən ðə ˈmid|ˈeidʒd| laik ˈjuː ən ˈmiː‖ ðɛəz ə ˈhjuːdʒ ˈdeindʒər| in riˈfjuːziŋ tuː əkˌnɔlidʒ| ðət ˈlɑːdʒ ˌisjuːz| ə ˈjuːʒ|i ˈkɔmpleks‖

ˈhjuː ai ˈdount riˌfjuːz tuː əkˌnɔlidʒ it| bət ai səˈdʒest ðət ˈdʒʌdʒmənts ʃud ˈnɔt biː əˈdʒʌstid| tə ˈsjuːt ðiː ˈeidʒ əv ðə ˈsʌbdʒikt‖ ˈvæljuːz ə ˈvæljuːz| ət ˈeni ˌeidʒ‖

ˈdʒɔːdʒ sou ə ˈfaiv jiər ˈould ˈtʃaild| ənd ə ˈnaintiːn jiər ˈould ˈstjuːdn̩t| ənd ə ˈmid| eidʒd ˈdʒentlmən laik ˈjuː ɔː ˈmiː| ʃud ˈɔːl bi ˈdʒʌdʒd əˈlaik‖

ˈhjuː ˈdount bi ˈstjuːpid ˌdʒɔːdʒ‖ wiə ˈnɔt ˈɑːgjuiŋ əbaut ˌfaiv jiər ·ouldz‖

ˈdʒɔːdʒ bət juː ˈwud əˈgriː| ðət wiː ˈhæv ə ˈdjuːti tuː ˈedjukeit ðəm‖

ˈhjuː jɔː ˈveri inˈdʒiːnjəs ˌdʒɔːdʒ‖ ˈjes| ən wiː ˈhæv ə ˈdjuːti tuː ˈedjukeit ˈkɔlidʒ ˌstjuːdn̩ts‖ sou ai ˈʃudn̩t ˈdʒʌdʒ ðə ˈjʌŋ| əz ai ˈdʒʌdʒ ˈjuː juː ˌeidʒiŋ ˌdʒent|mən‖

ˈdʒɔːdʒ ˈlets ˈtʃeindʒ ðə ˈsʌbdʒikt‖ ˈhæv juː ˈmænidʒd tuː əˈreindʒ jɔː ˌhɔlədiz ·jet‖

Examples   yet   jet   yours   jaws
                 dune   June   India   injure
                  use   juice   lawyer   Georgia

Hugh and George

George   Did you read John Young's page in Tuesday's *Guardian*? On European students?

Hugh   Yes, and it was a jolly useful contribution. John Young generally makes me furious, and I reject his views immediately as a hodge-podge of ill-digested pseudo-intellectual garbage. But yesterday's page was genuinely valuable, for a change. I enjoyed it.

George   Strange that *you* enjoyed it, Hugh, unless your views on students have changed. You're not usually very generous in your judgments of youth.

Hugh   Not generous? You're joking, George. I judge students, and other young people, with just as much generosity as I judge humanity in general. There's no excuse for changing one's values just because the subject is another age-group.

George   Yes, don't imagine I'm disparaging your judgment, Hugh, just challenging your use of the same yardstick for the younger generation and the middle-aged like you and me. There's a huge danger in refusing to acknowledge that large issues are usually complex.

Hugh   I don't refuse to acknowledge it, but I suggest that judgments should not be adjusted to suit the age of the subject. Values are values, at any age.

George   So a five-year old child and a nineteen-year old student and a middle-aged gentleman like you or me should all be judged alike.

Hugh   Don't be stupid, George. We are not arguing about five-year olds.

George   But you would agree that we have a duty to educate them?

Hugh   You're very ingenious, George. Yes, and we have a duty to educate college students, so I shouldn't judge the young as I judge you, you ageing gentleman.

George   Let's change the subject. Have you managed to arrange your holidays yet?

igˈzɑːmplz   ˈhɛə   ˈɛə   biˈheiv   bi ˈeibl
              ˈhedʒ   ˈedʒ   inˈheil   iˈnein
              ˈhɑːt   ˈɑːt   inˈhɑːns in ˈɑːnsə

ˈhenri ənd ˈeidriən

ˈhenri   ˈou| ˈeidriən‖ ˈwɔt ə ˈhæpi ˈæksidənt‖ aim ˈveri ˈæŋʃəs tə ˈhæv
         jɔːr ədˈvais‖ ˈɑː juː in ə ˌhʌri‖
ˈeidriən   ˈnɔt əˈtɔːl‖ ˈhau kən ai ˈhelp‖
ˈhenri   ˈhæv juː eni ˌhints tuː· ·ɔfər| ɔn ˈsentrəl ˌhiːtiŋ‖ aim ˈhoupiŋ tə
         biː ˈeibl tə ˌhæv it| in auə ˈnjuː ˈhaus‖
ˈeidriən   ˈɑː juː· ˈhæviŋ ə ˈnjuː ˌhaus‖ ai ˈhædn̩t ˈhəːd‖ ˈhiər in ˌæmhəːst‖
ˈhenri   ˈaiðə ˈhiər in ˇæmhəːst| in ˈhɔːtn̩ ˇævənjuː‖ ɔːr ˈʌp ɔn ðə ˈhil
         biˈhaind it‖ aiv ˈhæd ən ˈɔfər əv ˈhɑːf ən ˈeikər| in ðə ˈheihəːst
         ˌɛəriə‖
ˈeidriən   ai ˈhoup jɔː ˈhæviŋ ən ˇɑːkitekt‖
ˈhenri   ai ˇæm| bət ai ˈhævn̩t ˈeni aiˈdiə ˈhuː ˌjet‖ in ˈeni iˌvent| ðɛəz
         ˈnou ˈɔːf| ˇhʌri‖ aim ˈeimiŋ ˈeitiːn ˈmʌnθs əˈhed‖ hauˈevə| ai hæv
         ˈhʌndrədz əv aiˇdiəz| əbaut ˌhau ai ˇwɔnt it‖ ənd ai ˈɔbviəsli ˈɔːt tə
         kouˈɔːdineit ðəm| biˈfɔːr ai gou ˈaut ən ˈhaiər ən ˇɑːkitekt‖
ˈeidriən   ˈaivə ˈhjuːz wəz ˌɔːfli ˌhelpfl̩ tuː· ˌʌs‖
ˈhenri   hiːz ən ˈɑːkitekt| ˌiz iː‖ ai ˈhævn̩t ˈhəːd əv ˌhim‖
ˈeidriən   ˈou| ˌhævn̩t juː‖ hiː ˈhæz ən ˈɔfis in ðə ˈhai striːt‖
ˈhenri   ˈhau ˈould iz iː‖
ˈeidriən   in iz ˈəːli ˈfɔːtiz ai iˌmædʒən‖ ai ˈhævn̩t ˈɑːst im‖
ˈhenri   ˈou| hiː ˈizn̩t ðæt ˈintrəstiŋ ˈtʃæp huː inˈheritid ˈhauəd ˈæŋgəsiz
         ˌɔfis ˌiz iː‖
ˈeidriən   ˈou nou| hiz ˈɔfis iz ˈhaiər ˈʌp ðən ˌhauədz ·ould wʌn‖ ˈenihau|
         hiːz ən ˈeksələnt ˇɑːkitekt‖ bət ˈhau əbaut ðis ˈhiːtiŋ ju· ˌɑːst miː
         əˌbaut‖
ˈhenri   wel ˈhæviŋ ˈhəːd frəm ˇælis| huː· ˈhəːd it frəm ˇhelən| ðət juːd
         hæd ˈɔil ˈfaiəd ˌhiːtiŋ inˌstɔːld| in jɔːr ˈoun ˌhaus| ai ˈhoupt juːd biː
         ˈeibl tə ˈhelp‖
ˈeidriən   ai ˈhævn̩t hæd ˈeni ˈæktʃuəl ikˈspiəriəns əv ˌʌðə ·kainz əv
         ·hiːtiŋ| bət ˈhelən ənd ˌai| ˈdid inˈvestigeit ðə ˈhoul ˈhiːtiŋ pəˈziʃn̩|
         ˈveri ˈθʌrəli‖ ənd aid biː ˈounli ˈtuː ˈhæpi| tuː· ˌɔfə juː ˈeni ˈhints ai
         ˈkæn‖
ˈhenri   hau ˈveri ˈhænsəm ɔv juː‖

Examples   hair   air   behave   be able
            hedge   edge   inhale   inane
            heart   art   enhance   in answer

Henry and Adrian

Henry Oh, Adrian, what a happy accident. I'm very anxious to have your advice. Are you in a hurry?

Adrian Not at all. How can I help?

Henry Have you any hints to offer on central heating? I'm hoping to be able to have it in our new house.

Adrian Are you having a new house? I hadn't heard. Here in Amherst?

Henry Either here in Amherst, in Horton Avenue, or up on the hill behind it. I've had an offer of half an acre in the Hayhurst area.

Adrian I hope you're having an architect.

Henry I am, but I haven't any idea who yet. In any event, there's no awful hurry. I'm aiming eighteen months ahead. However, I have hundreds of ideas about how I want it and I obviously ought to coordinate them before I go out and hire an architect.

Adrian Ivor Hughes was awfully helpful to us.

Henry He's an architect, is he? I haven't heard of him.

Adrian Oh, haven't you? He has an office in the High Street.

Henry How old is he?

Adrian In his early forties, I imagine, I haven't asked him.

Henry Oh, he isn't that interesting chap who inherited Howard Angus's office, is he?

Adrian Oh no, his office is higher up than Howard's old one. Anyhow, he's an excellent architect. But how about this heating you asked me about?

Henry Well, having heard from Alice, who heard it from Helen, that you'd had oil-fired heating installed in your own house, I hoped you'd be able to help.

Adrian I haven't had any actual experience of other kinds of heating, but Helen and I did investigate the whole heating position very thoroughly, and I'd be only too happy to offer you any hints I can.

Henry How very handsome of you.

igˈzɑːmp|z   ˈpai   ˈbai   ˈberi   ˈveri
              ˈkʌp   ˈkʌb   ˈkəːb   ˈkəːv
              ˈsimp| ˈsimb| ˈhæbit ˈhæv it

ˈviviən ən ˈbɔb

ˈbɔb ˈviv| fə ˈhevn̩z ˈseik ˈstɔp ˈklæmbəriŋ əˈbaut ðə ˌpleis‖ its
ˈpɔzətivli ʌnˈnəːviŋ‖ juːv biːn ˈbæŋiŋ ə,baut| ˈevə sins ˈsʌpə‖
ˈviviən its mai ˈglʌvz‖ ðeiv ˈdisəˈpiəd| ən aim ˈbloud if ail ˈbai ə ˈnjuː
ˌpɛə‖ ai riˈmembə ˈputiŋ ðəm in ðə ˈbɔtəm əv ˈðis ˈkʌbəd‖ ˈjuː ˌhævn̩t
ˌmuːvd ðəm| ˌhæv juː‖
ˈbɔb ˈmuːvd ˈjɔː ˌglʌvz‖ ˈnou| əv ˈkɔːs ai ˌhævn̩t‖ ai ˈhævn̩t ˈiːvn̩ ˈklæpt
ˈaiz ɔn ðəm‖
ˈviviən ˈpræps it wəz ðə ˈtɔp ˌkʌbəd‖ ˈbiː ə ˌpet| ən ˈbriŋ ðə ˌsteps frəm
ðə ˌspɛə ˌbedrum‖
ˈbɔb ˈou ˈveri ˌwel‖ ai səˈpouz ail ˈnevə hæv eni ˇpiːs| ʌnˈtil juːv
diˈskʌvəd ðəm‖ ˈðɛə| ˈwʌn ˈpɛər əv ˈsteps‖
ˈviviən ˈklevə ˈbɔi‖ ˈhevn̩z əˈbʌv| ˈðis ˈkʌbədz in ən əˈpɔːliŋ ˌmes‖ its
ˈpɔzətivli riˈvoultiŋ‖ ˈbɔb| juːv ˈsimpli ˈgɔt tə ˈhelp miː tə ˈput it intə
ˈriːznəb| ˈʃeip‖
ˈbɔb ˈou ˈblɑːst ðə ˌkʌbəd| aim ˈriːdiŋ ðiː ˈiːvniŋ ˈpeipə‖
ˈviviən ˈbɔðə jɔː ˌpeipə‖ ˈstɔp biːiŋ əbˈstrʌktiv| ən ˈliːv it‖
ˈbɔb ˈnevər ən ˈiːvniŋ ˇpɑːsiz| bət juː prəˈvaid sʌm əˈbɔminəb| ˈdʒɔb
ˌfɔː miː‖
ˈviviən ˈpuə ˈbeibi‖ ˈhiə| ˈput ðis ˈræpiŋ ·peipər in ðə ˈbjuərou| wiːl ˈseiv
it fə ˈbəːθdi ˌprezn̩ts‖ ən ˈʃʌv ðis ˈrʌbiʃ in ðə ˈweis peipə ˌbɑːskit‖
its ə ˈprɔpə ˈʃæmb|z ʌp ˌhiə‖ ˈbɔt|d ˌæp|z| ˈruːbɑːb pri,zəːv| ˈrʌbə
ˌglʌvz| ˈbroukən ˌpen ·nibz| vəˈnilə ˌfleivəriŋ| ˌbeikiŋ ·paudə|
ˌpeint ·pɔts‖
ˈbɔb ˌpaint ·pɔts‖
ˈviviən ˈpeint pɔts ˌlʌv‖ bət ðɛər ˈɑː ˈsevn̩ ˈbiə ˌbɔt|z‖
ˈbɔb ˌbiə ·bɔt|z| ɔː ˈbɔt|z əv ˈbiə‖
ˈviviən ˈbouθ ai bə,liːv‖
ˈbɔb ai ˈhoup ˌsou‖ ˈpɑːs ðəm ˌouvə ·viv‖ ˈlʌvli| mai ˈfeivrət ˈbruː‖ ˈfaiv
ˇempti| bət ˈnevə ˌmaind‖ ˈlets hæv ə ˈbit əv ə ˈbreik| ənd ə ˈdrɔp əv
ˈbiə| tə riˈvaiv əs‖
ˈviviən aid ˈbetə put ˈʃelf ˌpeipər| ɔn ðiː ˈʌpə ˈʃelvz| bi,fɔː ˌgiviŋ ˌʌp‖
ˈpɑːs miː ə ˌbrʌʃ n̩ ˌʃʌv|‖
ˈbɔb ˈstɔp ˈbiːvəriŋ əˈbaut nau| juːl ˈbəːst ə ˈblʌd ˌves|‖
ˈviviən ˈprɔbəbli‖ bət riˈmembə ðət ˈwaivz liv ˈlɔŋgə ðən ˌhʌzbəndz|
ɔn ˌævridʒ‖
ˈbɔb pjuəli biˈkɔz ðei ˈliːv ðə ˈhevi dʒɔbz tə ðɛə ˇhʌzbəndz‖
ˈviviən ˈjuːv gɔt ə ˌnəːv juː ·vilən‖

Examples   pie   buy   berry   very
              cup   cub   curb   curve
              simple   symbol   habit   have it

Vivienne and Bob

Bob Viv, for heaven's sake stop clambering about the place. It's positively unnerving. You've been banging about ever since supper.

Vivienne It's my gloves. They've disappeared and I'm blowed if I'll buy a new pair. I remember putting them in the bottom of this cupboard. You haven't moved them, have you?

Bob Moved your gloves? No, of course I haven't; I haven't even clapped eyes on them.

Vivienne Perhaps it was the top cupboard. Be a pet and bring the steps from the spare bedroom.

Bob Oh, very well. I suppose I'll never have any peace until you've discovered them. There, one pair of steps.

Vivienne Clever boy. Heavens above! This cupboard's in an appalling mess. It's positively revolting! Bob, you've simply got to help me to put it into reasonable shape.

Bob Oh, blast the cupboard, I'm reading the evening paper.

Vivienne Bother your paper. Stop being obstructive and leave it.

Bob Never an evening passes but you provide some abominable job for me.

Vivienne Poor baby! Here, put this wrapping paper in the bureau, we'll save it for birthday presents. And shove this rubbish in the waste-paper basket. It's a proper shambles up here. Bottled apples, rhubarb preserve, rubber gloves, broken pen nibs, vanilla flavouring, baking powder, paint pots . . .

Bob Pint pots?

Vivienne Paint pots, love. But there are seven beer bottles.

Bob Beer bottles, or bottles of beer?

Vivienne Both, I believe.

Bob I hope so. Pass them over, Viv. Lovely, my favourite brew. Five empty, but never mind. Let's have a bit of a break and a drop of beer to revive us.

Vivienne I'd better put shelf paper on the upper shelves before giving up. Pass me a brush and shovel.

Bob Stop beavering about, now. You'll burst a blood vessel.

Vivienne Probably. But remember that wives live longer than husbands on average.

Bob Purely because they leave the heavy jobs to their husbands.

Vivienne You've got a nerve, you villain.

 igˈzɑːmp|z   ˈtouz   ˈdouz   ˈðouz
              ˈrait   ˈraid   ˈraið
              ˈsiːtiŋ   ˈsiːdiŋ   ˈsiːðiŋ

ˈheðər ən ˈtedi

ˈtedi   wiːv ˈdefnətli diˈsaidid tə ˈhould ðis ˈpɑːti in ðə ˈgɑːdn̩| ˌrɑːðə
ðən inˌdɔːz| ˌhæv wiː‖

ˈheðə   ˈsəːtn̩li‖ it wud bi ˈmædnəs tə ˌtrai ənd entəˌtein ˌɔːl ðouz
ˌtʃildrən inˌdɔːz‖ ðɛəz ˈbaund tə biː ə triˈmendəs ˌkraud| ən ðeid
ˈtɛə ðə ˈflæt tə ˈbits| ʌnˈdautidli‖

ˈtedi   ˈwɔt ˈsɔːt əv ˌkraud‖ ˌtwenti| ˌfifti| ə ˌhʌndrəd‖

ˈheðə   wel its ˈɔːl ðə ˇkidz| huːv ˈhæd ˈauəz tə ˌtiː ˌleitli‖ ˈlets ˈsit ˈdaun
ən ˈrait ə ˈlist‖

ˈtedi   ˈðæts ə ˌgud aiˌdiə| bət ˈwɔt ˈtaim ʃud it ˈstɑːt‖

ˈheðə   ˈkudn̩t wiː ˈlet ðæt ˈweit til ˌleitə‖ wiː ˈniːd tə diˈsaid ˇfəːst| ˈweðə
ðeil ˈɔːl ˈfit intə ðə ˈgɑːdn̩ ɔː ˌnɔt‖ ənd ˈif ˇnɔt| ˈweðə tə ˈtrim ðə ˇlist|
ɔː tə ˈsplit ðəm| biˌtwiːn ˈtuː ˈdifrənt ˈdeiz‖

ˈtedi   ai ˈʃudn̩t ˈwɔnt tə ˈduː ˇðæt‖ ai ˈlouð ðə ˌθɔːt əv ˌðis| ət ðə ˈbest‖
ənd it wud ˈdraiv miː ˈmæd tə ˌduː it ˌtwais‖

ˈheðə   ˇtruː| bət wiː ˈdid diˈsaid ət ði: ˈautset| ˈdidnt wiː| ðət ði: ˈɔːdiəl
ˈhæd tə biː inˈdjuəd‖ ənd if ðei ˈkɑːnt bi ˈfitid ˈin ɔn ˈwʌn ˌdei| wiː
ʃ| ˈniːd tuː ikˈstend it tuː əˈnʌðə‖

ˈtedi   ˈrait| bət ˈwɔts tə bi ˌdʌn| if ðə ˈweðə ˌlets əs ˌdaun‖

ˈheðə   ai ˈdɛənt ˈkɔntəmˌpleit it‖ wiˈðaut ˈdiːsn̩t ˇweðə| ðə ˈθiŋ ˈkudn̩t
bi ˈdʌn‖

ˈtedi   ðə ˈflæt ˈwudn̩t ˈhould ə ˈtenθ əv ðəm| ən ˈðen ˌhɑːf əv ðəm wud
bi ˌfɔːst tə ˌbriːð ˌin‖ wailst ði: ˌʌðəz wə ˌbriːðiŋ ˌaut‖

ˈheðə   ˈnɔt ə ˈbæd aiˈdiə ˌðæt‖ ˈsmʌðə ðə ˈlɔt ə ðəm‖

ˈtedi   ˌidiət‖ ai ˈwʌndə ˈweðə . . .

ˈheðə   ˈweðə ˈwɔt‖

ˈtedi   ai ˈwʌndə ˈweðə wiː kud ˈteik ðəm tə ðə ˈzuː‖

ˈheðə   ˈðæts ə triˈmendəs aiˌdiə‖ wiː kud ˈgæðə ðəm təˈgeðər ət ðə
ˌsteiʃn̩| ˈteik ˈtiː ˌwið əs| ən ˈdɔdʒ inˈdɔːz if ðə ˌweðə ·təːnd ·bæd‖
ˈdount ˈbɔðə wið ˌðæt ˌlist‖ ˈlet ðəm ˈkʌm in ðɛə ˈhʌndrədz‖

Examples	toes	doze	those
	right	ride	writhe
	seating	seeding	seething

Heather and Teddy

Teddy We've definitely decided to hold this party in the garden rather than indoors, have we?

Heather Certainly. It would be madness to try and entertain all those children indoors. There's bound to be a tremendous crowd and they'd tear the flat to bits, undoubtedly.

Teddy What sort of a crowd? Twenty, fifty, a hundred?

Heather Well it's all the kids that have had ours to tea lately. Let's sit down and write a list.

Teddy That's a good idea, but what time should it start?

Heather Couldn't we let that wait till later? We need to decide first whether they'll all fit into the garden or not, and if not, whether to trim the list or to split them between two different days.

Teddy I shouldn't want to do that. I loathe the thought of this at the best, and it would drive me mad to do it twice.

Heather True, but we did decide at the outset, didn't we, that the ordeal had to be endured, and if they can't be fitted in on one day, then we shall need to extend it to another.

Teddy Right. But what's to be done if the weather lets us down?

Heather I daren't contemplate it. Without decent weather the thing couldn't be done.

Teddy The flat wouldn't hold a tenth of them, and then half of them would be forced to breathe in whilst the others were breathing out.

Heather Not a bad idea, that; smother the lot of them.

Teddy Idiot! I wonder whether . . .

Heather Whether what?

Teddy I wonder whether we could take them to the zoo.

Heather That's a tremendous idea! We could gather them together at the station, take tea with us, and dodge indoors if the weather turned bad. Don't bother with that list, let them come in their hundreds.

ig`zaːmp|z     `keit   `geit       `koul   `goul
            `bæk    `bæg   `lɔk    `lɔg
            `æŋk|   `æŋg| `bikə   `bigə

                     `keit ən `gregəri

`keit   `ou| `greg‖ θæŋk `gudnəs juːv `gɔt `bæk| ai wəz bi`giniŋ tə
   `pænik‖
`gregəri    `gud `greiʃəs ˌkeit| juː luk `kwait di`stræktid‖ `wɔts ðə `greit
   `kraisis‖
`keit    fə `gɔdz `seik `gou ən `græb ðə `dɔg‖ hiːz `gɔn `neks `dɔːr| ənd iːz
   `kɔːziŋ `hævək| in ðə `klegz `gaːdn̩ əˌgen‖
`gregəri    `gud `griːf| `kaːnt ðei `kiːp ðɛə ˌgeit ·lɔkt‖ juːd `θiŋk wið ə
   `pedigriː ˇkæt| ðeid `teik `kɛə ðət `dogz `kudn̩t get `in‖
`keit    its `nou `gud ˇgrʌmb|iŋ| `gou ən `koup wið im‖ ail `get juː ə `big
   `driŋk wen juː ˌget ˌbæk‖
   (`ten `minits `leitə)
`gregəri    `kwik| `klouz ðə `bæk `dɔː‖ `gud ˌdɔg| `kwaiət ˌnau‖ `giv miː
   iz `kɔlə‖ `mai `gudnəs| `wɔt ə `strʌg|‖
`keit    ail `get juː ə `glaːs əv `wiski‖ it tuk juː `lɔŋgə ðən ai ik`spektid‖
`gregəri    `θæŋks ˌkeit‖ it wəz `keiɔs‖ aim kəm`pliːtli ´ig`zɔːstid‖
`keit    `wəː ðə `klegz ˌæŋgri‖
`gregəri    ˇæŋgri‖ wen `ai gɔt ˌðɛə| `dʒæk ˌkleg| həd `gɔt iz `fiŋgər ɔn ðə
     `trigər əv iz `gʌn‖ `tuː ˇsekənz| ən ðə `dɔg wud əv `biːn ə `gɔnə‖ ai
     ə`griː ðə ˌgaːdn̩ ˌlukt laik ə ˌrek| ən ðə ˌdɔg əd ˌgɔt ðɛə ˌkæt ˌkɔːnəd|
     əˌgenst ðə ˌbæk ˌgeit‖ bət ai `aːsk juː‖ ə `gʌn| ə`genst ə `dɔg‖
`keit    ðə `big `pig‖ ail `nevə `spiːk tə ðə `klegz ə`gen‖
`gregəri    `ou| `pegi wɔznt ˌæŋgri‖ ˇæktʃəli| ai `θiŋk ʃiː wəz `tik|d ˇpiŋk|
     ðət ðə `dɔg əd `broukən ðæt `gaːstli `pəːgələr əv ˌdʒæks‖
`keit    `kwait `laikli‖ ʃiː `nevə ˇlaikt it‖
`gregəri    ənd `dʒæk `kuːld `ɔf| wen ai ˌgɔt ðə ˌdɔg bai ðə ˌskrʌf ə ðə
     ˌnek| ən ðə `kæt iˇskeipt‖ hiː ri`gretid ðət ðə `geit `wɔznt ˇklouzd|
     ənd `ai əˇgriːd| ðət wiːd `kiːp ðə ˌdɔg| ʌndə `klousə kən`troul‖
`keit    θæŋk `gudnəs juː `gɔt `bæk in ðə `nik əv `taim‖ bət `tɔːkiŋ əv ðə
     ˇdɔg| `wɛəz ðə `begə `gɔt tuː `nau‖
`gregəri    `ou| mai `gɔd‖ hiːz `gɔn əˌgen‖ `ai giv `ʌp‖

Examples   Kate   gate   coal   goal
              back   bag   lock   log
              ankle   angle   bicker bigger

Kate and Gregory

Kate Oh, Greg, thank goodness you've got back. I was beginning to panic.

Gregory Gracious, Kate, you look quite distracted. What's the great crisis?

Kate For God's sake go and grab the dog. He's gone next door and he's causing havoc in the Cleggs' garden again.

Gregory Good grief! Can't they keep their gate locked? You'd think with a pedigree cat they'd take care that dogs couldn't get in.

Kate It's no good grumbling. Go and cope with him. I'll get you a big drink when you get back.

(*Ten minutes later*)

Gregory Quick. Close the back door. Good dog. Quiet now. Give me his collar. My goodness! What a struggle!

Kate I'll get you a glass of whisky. It took you longer than I expected.

Gregory Thanks, Kate. It was chaos. I'm completely exhausted.

Kate Were the Cleggs angry?

Gregory Angry? When I got there Jack Clegg had got his finger on the trigger of his gun. Two seconds and the dog would have been a goner. I agree the garden looked like a wreck and the dog had got their cat cornered against the back gate. But I ask you! A gun against a dog!

Kate The big pig! I'll never speak to the Cleggs again.

Gregory Oh, Peggy wasn't angry. Actually, I think she was tickled pink that the dog had broken that ghastly pergola of Jack's.

Kate Quite likely. She never liked it.

Gregory And Jack cooled off when I got the dog by the scruff of the neck and the cat escaped. He regretted that the gate wasn't closed, and I agreed that we'd keep the dog under closer control.

Kate Thank goodness you got back in the nick of time, but talking of the dog, where's the beggar got to now?

Gregory Oh my God! He's gone again. I give up.

ig΄zɑːmp|z   ΄vəːs   ΄wəːs   ΄vain   ΄wain
            ə΄veil   ə ΄weil   ΄aivi   ΄haiwei
            ΄weivəd   ΄weiwəd   ΄gɑːvin   ΄dɑːwin

ðə ΄vikəz ΄wɔtʃ

΄vikə iz ΄ðæt ΄weivəli ΄wʌn ΄faiv ΄faiv ˏwʌn‖ ɑː ΄juː ˏvænwəlz| ðə ˏwɔtʃ
·piːpl‖ . . . ΄mai ΄neim iz ΄weiv|‖ aim ΄vikər əv ΄waivən| ənd ai ΄wɔnt
tuː iŋ΄kwaiər əbaut ə ΄wɔtʃ aiv biːn ˏgivn‖ ai bi΄liːv its ΄veri ΄væljuəbl|
ənd ai ΄wʌndəd weðə ΄vænwəlz wud bi ΄wiliŋ tə ΄bai it‖ . . . ΄jes| ΄veri
ˏvæljuəbl‖ ai ΄wud əv ΄givn it əˏwei| bət mai ΄waif wount ΄hiər əv it‖
ənd aiv ΄ləːnt ouvə ðə ˇjiəz| tə giv ΄greit ΄weit tə mai ˏwaifs ·vjuːz‖
həːr əd΄vais iz in΄vɛəriəbli ΄waiz‖ . . . ΄wɔt ˏkaind əv ·wɔtʃ‖ . . . wel its
ə ΄self΄waindiŋ ΄swis wʌn| ənd its ˏmeid əv ə ˏsɔːt əv ΄wouvn ΄silvə
ˏwəːk| wið ΄hevi ΄gould ΄veinz| ɔn ðə ri΄vəːs‖ ΄ouvər ənd ə΄bʌv ˇwitʃ|
it hæz ΄evri kən΄siːvəbl| ΄gædʒit‖ ai bi΄liːv its ΄wəːθ ΄wel ouvə ΄faiv
΄hʌndrəd‖ . . . ΄wai duː ai ΄wɔnt tə ˏsel it‖ . . . wel ai wəz ΄givn it əz ə
ri΄wɔːd| fə ΄seiviŋ ðə ΄laif əv ə ΄jʌŋ ΄wumən‖ ʃiː ΄ouvə΄təːnd ə ΄kærəvæn|
in ðə ΄rivə ΄wai| ənd ΄ai ΄daivd ΄in| ən ΄seivd həː‖ ΄vəːtjuː iz its ΄oun
ri΄wɔːd əv ˏkɔːs| bət həː ˇhʌzbənd| iz wʌn əv ðə ΄ritʃist ΄men in ðə
΄west‖ ənd ΄æz hiː wəz ΄veri mʌtʃ in ΄lʌv wið iz ˏwaif| hiː ΄wud
ri΄wɔːd miː| bai ΄giviŋ miː ðis ΄lʌvli ΄wɔtʃ‖ . . . aim ΄wel ə΄wɛər əv
ˏðæt| it wəz ΄veri ˏsiv| ɔv im‖ bət ai ΄dount ΄wɔnt it‖ ai kud ΄nevə
ˇwɛər it| ai ΄wudnt hæv ðə ΄nəːv‖ sou ΄wɔt ai ˇwɔnt| iz tə kən΄vəːt it
intə ΄kæʃ| ənd ə΄kwaiər ə ΄væn‖ aiv ΄ɔːlwiz ˏwɔntid ə ˏvæn| fə mai
΄wəːk| bət aiv ΄nevər əˇtʃiːvd wʌn‖ ΄biːiŋ ðə ΄vikər əv ˇwaivən| aiv
΄kwait ə ΄waid ΄ɛəriə tə ˏkʌvə‖ . . . juː ˏwil‖ ΄witʃ ΄dei‖ . . . ΄wenzdi
bitwiːn ΄twelv ən ΄wʌn‖ ΄wʌndəf|‖ aim ΄veri ΄greitf|‖ ΄gudˏbai‖

Examples	verse	worse	vine	wine
	avail	a whale	ivy	highway
	wavered	wayward	Garvin	Darwin

The Vicar's Watch

Vicar Is that Waverley 1551? Are you Vanwell's, the watch people?
...My name is Wavell, I'm vicar of Wyvern and I want to enquire
about a watch I've been given. I believe it's very valuable and I wondered whether Vanwell's would be willing to buy it...Yes, very
valuable. I would have given it away but my wife won't hear of it, and
I've learned over the years to give great weight to my wife's views.
Her advice is invariably wise... What kind of watch?... Well, it's a
self-winding Swiss one, and it's made of a sort of woven silver-work,
with heavy gold veins on the reverse. Over and above which, it has
every conceivable gadget. I believe it's worth well over five hundred....
Why do I want to sell it? Well, I was given it as a reward for saving
the life of a young woman. She overturned a caravan in the River
Wye, and I dived in and saved her. Virtue is its own reward, of
course, but her husband is one of the wealthiest men in the West,
and as he was very much in love with his wife he would reward me
by giving me this lovely watch... I'm well aware of that, it was very
civil of him. But I don't want it. I could never wear it, I wouldn't
have the nerve. So what I want is to convert it into cash and acquire
a van. I've always wanted a van for my work, but I've never achieved
one. Being the vicar of Wyvern I've quite a wide area to cover... You
will? Which day?...Wednesday, between twelve and one. Wonderful. I'm very grateful. Goodbye.

ig'zɑːmp|z	'hæŋə	'æŋgə	'æŋkə	'sʌm	'sʌn	'sʌŋ
	'lɔŋiŋ	'lɔŋgə	'kɔŋkə	'wim	'win	'wiŋ
	'siŋə	'liŋgə	'piŋkə	'rʌm	'rʌn	'rʌŋ

'mounər ən 'fræŋk

'fræŋk   'ɑː juː in'tendiŋ tə gou ,ʃɔpiŋ ðis ·mɔːniŋ‖

'mounə   ai 'θiŋk ,sou| bət ðə 'wɔʃiŋz ,teikiŋ miː ,lɔŋgə ðən ai ,bɑːgənd ·fɔː‖ ðə 'riŋəz nɔt ,wəːkiŋ fə ,sʌm ·riːzŋ| ənd aim 'hæviŋ tə 'riŋ 'evriθiŋ bai 'hænd‖

'fræŋk   ai wəz 'wʌndriŋ if juː kud 'gou ə'lɔŋ tə 'jʌŋgəz| ði: 'aiənmʌŋgəz| ən 'briŋ miː səm 'æŋg| ,aiənz‖

'mounə 'wɔt ər 'æŋg| ,aiənz ,wen ðɛər ət ,houm‖

'fræŋk   ðɛə 'met| 'pousts| fə sə'pɔːtiŋ ,θiŋz‖ aim 'plæniŋ tə 'streŋθən ðə 'fens in ðə 'frʌnt 'gɑːdŋ| ənd 'æŋg| aiənz wud biː ðə mous 'sensəb| 'θiŋ‖

'mounə   'dʌz it ,niːd ·streŋθəniŋ‖

'fræŋk   'jes| 'sʌm ə ðə 'wudŋ 'pousts ə 'rɔtiŋ| ən ðə 'neks 'strɔŋ ˇwind| mait ,briŋ ðə 'houl 'dæmd 'θiŋ ,daun‖ sou if ai kən 'bæŋ in səm 'æŋg| ,aiənz| ai kən 'æŋkə ðə 'wudŋ 'pousts ,tuː ðəm| ən pri'vent ðəm 'breikiŋ‖

'mounə   'wen də juː 'wɔnt ðəm‖

'fræŋk   ai wəz 'θiŋkiŋ əv biˇginiŋ it| ðis 'kʌmiŋ 'sʌndi‖

'mounə   'ou| ðɛəz 'plenti əv ,taim ðen‖ 'wai nɔt trai 'founiŋ ,jʌŋgəz| ənd ik'spleiniŋ wɔt juː 'wɔnt‖ 'ðen ai 'ʃɑːnt biː 'hæŋiŋ ə'baut 'tuː 'lɔŋ 'weitiŋ ,fɔː ðəm‖

'fræŋk   ai 'kɑːnt ,foun ðəm‖ ai miːn ai 'traid 'sʌm 'taim ,sins| ən ðɛə wəz 'nou 'ɑːnsə‖ ðə 'foun 'simpli 'kept ɔn 'riŋiŋ ənd 'riŋiŋ‖

'mounə   'trai 'founiŋ ə'gen| it 'mei əv biːn ə 'rɔŋ 'nʌmbə‖

'fræŋk   ai 'dount 'θiŋk ,sou‖ ai 'ræŋ 'mɔː ðən 'wʌns| ən ðə 'seim 'θiŋ ,hæpənd‖

'mounə   'dʌznt it 'meik juː 'æŋgri‖ ðɛə 'mʌs biː ,sʌmwən bi,hain ðə ,kauntər| ət ,ðis ·taim ə ðə ·mɔːniŋ

'fræŋk   'ðæts wai ai 'wʌndəd if juː wə 'gouiŋ 'ʃɔpiŋ‖

'mounə   ai 'θiŋk ail 'gou 'ɑːftə 'lʌnʃ ,nau‖ əz 'suːn əz aiv 'finiʃt ðə ,wɔʃiŋ| ail 'meik ən 'ɔmlət ɔː ,sʌmθiŋ‖ 'ɑː juː ,hʌŋgri‖

'fræŋk   'hʌŋgri əz ə 'hʌntə‖ 'θæŋk juː ,dɑːliŋ‖

Examples	hanger	anger	anchor	sum	sun	sung
	longing	longer	conquer	whim	win	wing
	singer	linger	pinker	rum	run	rung

Mona and Frank

Frank Are you intending to go shopping this morning?

Mona I think so, but the washing's taking me longer than I bargained for. The wringer's not working for some reason and I'm having to wring everything by hand.

Frank I was wondering if you could go along to Younger's, the iron-monger's, and bring me some angle-irons.

Mona What are angle-irons, when they're at home?

Frank They're metal posts for supporting things. I'm planning to strengthen the fence in the front garden, and angle-irons would be the most sensible thing.

Mona Does it need strengthening?

Frank Yes. Some of the wooden posts are rotting, and the next strong wind might bring the whole damned thing down. So if I can bang in some angle-irons, I can anchor the wooden posts to them and prevent them breaking.

Mona When do you want them?

Frank I was thinking of beginning it this coming Sunday.

Mona Oh, there's plenty of time, then. Why not try phoning Younger's and explaining what you want; then I shan't be hanging about too long waiting for them.

Frank I can't phone them. I mean, I tried some time since and there was no answer. The phone simply kept on ringing and ringing.

Mona Try phoning again; it may have been a wrong number.

Frank I don't think so. I rang more than once and the same thing happened.

Mona Doesn't it make you angry! There must be someone behind the counter at this time of the morning.

Frank That's why I wondered if you were going shopping.

Mona I think I'll go after lunch now. As soon as I've finished the washing I'll make an omelette or something. Are you hungry?

Frank Hungry as a hunter. Thank you, darling.

ig'zɑːmpļz   'red   'led   'rein   'lein
                  'terə   'telə   'beri   'beli
                  'kraim   'klaim   'prei   'plei

'rɔzəlind ən 'læri

'læri ˇrɔzəlind| aiv 'ræʃli ə'griːd tə 'draiv in ə 'kɑː ˌræli| ɔn ði ə'levņθ
əv 'eiprəl‖
'rɔzəlind ə ˇræli‖ aiv 'nevər ʌndə'stud ˌræliz‖ 'tel mi 'hau ðɛər
ə'reindʒd‖
'læri ðɛər in'vɛəriəbli ə'reindʒd bai ə 'moutriŋ ˌklʌb| hu: pri'pɛər ə
ˌruːt‖ 'dʒenrəli 'rɑːðər ə 'triki ˌruːt| θru: 'litļ 'leinz in ðə 'kʌntri‖
ən ði: ai'diər ˇiz| tə 'fɔlou ðə ˌruːt| 'æbsəluːtli 'ækjərətli‖ riˌlaiiŋ
in'taiəli ɔn ði: in'strʌkʃņz prə'vaidid‖ witʃ ə ˇjuːʒļi| 'veri 'difəkļt ən
'kɔmpliˌkeitid‖
'rɔzəlind ən 'juː ˇdraivəz| 'rɔːr ə'raund ðouz 'nærou 'kʌntri ˇleinz|
tə ðə 'terəb| 'perəl əv 'evriwən 'els| ən ðə 'θʌrə disə'pruːv| əv ðə
'louk| pə'liːs‖
'læri 'lɔːd ˌnou‖ ðə 'ruːlz ər ik'striːmli 'strikt‖ 'evri 'θriː ɔ: 'fɔː ˇmailz|
ðɛər ə kən'troulz‖ ən jɔ: ˇpiːnəlaizd| fər əˌraiviŋ ˌaiðər 'əːli ɔ: 'leit
ˌæt ðəm‖ sou ðə 'dʒenrəl ˇspiːd| iz 'veri 'rigərəsli kən'trould‖ ði:
'ouvərɔːl 'ævridʒ fə 'ðis pəˌtikjələ ˌræli| iz 'twenti 'θriː 'mailz pər
'auə‖ sou ðɛəz ˌæbsəluːtli 'nou 'riːzņ tə 'draiv ˇdeindʒrəsli‖
'rɔzəlind ðæts 'ɔːl veri 'welļ bət 'huːz 'kɑːr ə juː ˌdraiviŋ‖
'læri auər 'oun‖ its ˌriːznəbli rəˌlaiəb‖ ɑːftər 'ɔːlļ ðə 'gærɑːʒ ˌpiːpļ
wə 'riːznəbli riːə'ʃuəriŋ| ˌɑːftə ðæt ˌlɑːst ˌouvəhɔːl‖
'rɔzəlind 'ou| 'rʌbiʃ‖ its ə 'terəbļ ould ˌkreit| ən it 'rætļz laik ə 'ketļ
ˌdrʌm‖ it | 'never ə'raiv ət ðə 'fəːs kən'troul‖ it | 'breik 'daun| ən
'juːl 'trai tə ri'pɛər it| ən 'ðen 'draiv laik ə ˇluːnətik| tu: ə'raiv ət ðə
kən'troul in 'taim‖ ai 'θʌrəli 'disə'pruːv əv ðə 'houl 'prɔdʒekt‖
'læri bət 'rɔzəlind| 'dɑːliŋ‖ aiv ɔːl'redi 'prɔmist 'lɔrəns 'raili ðət ail
ˌdraiv im‖
'rɔzəlind 'lɔrəns ˌraili‖ 'izņt 'hi: ðæt 'tɔːl ˌblɔnd ·felou| 'terəbli 'gud
ˌlukiŋ| ən 'lʌvli 'dimpļz| 'wen i: 'smailz‖
'læri 'hau ik'strɔːdnərəli 'lirikļ‖| bət 'ðæts 'lɔrəns ɔːlˌrait‖
'rɔzəlind aiv 'dʒʌst ˇriəlaizd| aiv hæd ðə 'rɔŋ ai'diər əˌbaut ˌræliz‖
'præps ail 'kʌm ə'lɔŋ fə ðə 'raid‖

Examples	red	led	rain	lane
	terror	teller	berry	belly
	crime	climb	pray	play

Rosalind and Larry

Larry   Rosalind, I've rashly agreed to drive in a car rally on the eleventh of April.

Rosalind   A rally? I've never understood rallies. Tell me how they're arranged.

Larry   They're invariably, arranged by a motoring club who prepare a route, generally rather a tricky route through little lanes in the country, and the idea is to follow the route absolutely accurately, relying entirely on the instructions provided, which are usually very difficult and complicated.

Rosalind   And you drivers roar around those narrow country lanes to the terrible peril of everyone else, and the thorough disapproval of the local police.

Larry   Lord, no. The rules are extremely strict; every three or four miles there are controls, and you're penalised for arriving either early or late at them; so the general speed is very rigorously controlled. The overall average for this particular rally is twenty-three miles per hour, so there's absolutely no reason to drive dangerously.

Rosalind   That's all very well, but whose car are you driving?

Larry   Our own. It's reasonably reliable, after all. The garage people were reasonably reassuring after that last overhaul.

Rosalind   Oh rubbish! It's a terrible old crate and it rattles like a kettle drum. It'll never arrive at the first control. It'll break down and you'll try to repair it, and then drive like a lunatic to arrive at the control in time. I thoroughly disapprove of the whole project.

Larry   But Rosalind, darling, I've already promised Laurence Reilly that I'll drive him.

Rosalind   Laurence Reilly? Isn't he that tall, blond fellow? Terribly good-looking, and lovely dimples when he smiles?

Larry   How extraordinarily lyrical! But that's Laurence all right.

Rosalind   I've just realised I've had the wrong idea about rallies. Perhaps I'll come along for the ride.

'stjuːət ən ˈgreiəm

ˈstjuːət   'did juː 'mænidʒ tə 'finiʃ ðæt ˌfilm skript in ·gud ·taim‖

ˈgreiəm   ˈou ˌjes‖ in 'fækt ai 'finiʃt it ɔn ðə 'tenθ əv ɔkˈtoubə| wið
          'ɔːlmoust 'θriː 'wiːks tə ˈspɛə‖

ˈstjuːət   'ðæt wəz ˈsplendid‖ wen wiː ˈlɑːst ˌtɔːkt ə·baut it| juː ˌθɔːt ðət
          it 'prɔbəbli 'kudn̩t bi ˇdʌn| in 'les ðən ˈsiks ˈmʌnθs‖

ˈgreiəm   ðæts ˈkwait ˈrait‖ ənd ət ˇtaimz| it 'ɔːlmoust 'drouv miː ˈkreizi‖
          bət 'kris 'helpt miː triˈmendəsli‖ ʃiː 'taipt ðə ˌtekst| ənd 'kept ðə
          ˌflæt·kwaiət| 'tuk ðə 'kidz aut fə ˌwɔː ks ən ·sou ɔn| ənd 'brɔːt ˈkʌps əv
          ˈkɔfi| ɔː 'glɑːsiz əv ˈskwɔʃ| ət ðiː ə'proupriət ˈtaimz‖ ˈænd 'fuːd 'tuː
          əf ˌkɔːs‖ ai ˈiːt ˌmʌtʃ ˌmɔː sins ai ˌstɔpt ˌsmoukiŋ‖

ˈstjuːət   juː ˌdount ˌluk əz if juː ˌhæv ə ˌweit ·prɔbləm‖

ˈgreiəm   ai ˈdidn̩t ˌwailst ai ˌsmoukt| bət 'ðen mai ˈweistlain ˌstɑːtid tə
          ˌbʌldʒ| 'kwait diˈstiŋktli‖ ənd mai ˈklouðz didn̩t ˌfit miː‖

ˈstjuːət   'midḷ eidʒd ˈspred‖ ˌei‖

ˈgreiəm   igˈzæktli‖ ənd ai ˈkudn̩t əˈfɔːd tə get ˌnjuː ˌsuːts ənd ·θiŋz‖ sou
          ai di'saidid tuː ˈiːt ˌslaitli ˌles‖ 'ðæt 'wəːkt 'kwait ˈkwikli‖

ˈstjuːət   it ˈsəːtn̩li ˇhelps‖ bət tə 'get 'bæk tə ˈðis ˈfilm ˌskript‖ 'iz it ən
          əˈridʒin̩| ˌstɔːri| ɔː 'did juː əˈdæpt ˈsʌmbdi ˈelsiz‖

ˈgreiəm   ˈou| its ən 'ædæp'teiʃn̩ əv ə ˈθrilə| bai 'fræŋk ˈstreindʒlʌv|
          kɔːld 'laitniŋ 'ɔːlwiz 'straiks ˈtwais‖ 'hæv juː ˌred ·streindʒlʌvz
          ·stɔːriz ə·tɔːl‖

ˈstjuːət   ai 'dount ˇθiŋk sou‖ ˈwɔts ðə ˈsʌbdʒikt‖

ˈgreiəm   its əˈbaut ðis ˇtʃæp| huː 'wɔnts tə 'kil hiz 'welθi ˈɑːnt‖ sou hiː
          'riːkənˈstrʌkts ən ˈæksidn̩t hiː ˌwʌns ˌwitnəst‖

ˈstjuːət   ənd 'ðæts hau ðə 'laitniŋ 'straiks ˈtwais ai ˌspouz‖

ˈgreiəm   kəˈrekt‖ in ˈmai ˌvjuː| its ə ˈstjuːpid ˌsɔːt əv ˌplɔt| bət juː
          'kɑːnt ˈkwɔrḷ wið jɔː 'bred n̩ ˈbʌtə| ənd ai 'θiŋk aiv 'mænidʒd tə meik
          ˈmoust əv ðə ˌkærəktəz| 'kwait ˈhjuːmən‖

ˈstjuːət   ˈgreit‖ bət 'iznt ·it 'sʌmθiŋ əv ə ˌweist| fər ə 'tʃæp wið ˈjɔː
          ˌtælənt| tə bi 'tækḷiŋ 'hæk 'dʒɔbz laik ˌðæt‖

ˈgreiəm   ðə 'trʌbḷ ˇiz| ðət ai 'dount ˈmeik mʌtʃ frəm mai ˌsiəriəs ·wəːk‖
          sou ˈskript ˌraitiŋ| 'peiz ðə ˈbilz‖ aim ˈnɔt wʌn əv ðouz ˌɑːtists| huː
          'θraivz ɔn stɑːˈveiʃn̩‖

ˈstjuːət   ˌnou| bət 'dʌzn̩t it teik 'tuː mʌtʃ əv jɔː ˌtaim‖ if juː ˌspend
          'nain 'tenθs əv jɔː 'laif ɔn ˇfilmz| ðɛər 'iznt ˈmʌtʃ ˇleft| fə jɔː 'nɔvḷz ənd
          ˈpouimz‖

ˈgreiəm   ou its 'nɔt 'nain ˇtenθs‖ 'nɔt 'mɔː ðən ˈhɑːf‖ sou aiv ˈplenti əv
          ˌtaim| fə mai ˈʌðə ˌstʌf‖ biˈsaidz| it 'meiks ə ˈtʃeindʒ‖ ai 'kwait
          inˈdʒɔi it ˌmoustli‖ ðen 'wen aiv ˇfiniʃt| ai kən 'get 'bæk tə mai
          ˇnɔvḷz| riˈfreʃt ənd ˈstreŋθənd‖

ˈstjuːət   juː 'dount 'kiːp ˈbouθ ˌgouiŋ‖

ˈgreiəm   ˈnou| ai 'faind 'ðæt 'præktikli imˈpɔsəbl‖ it 'siːmz əz ðou ˈwʌn
          ˌkaind əv ˌraitiŋ| əbˈstrʌkts ðiː ˈʌðə‖ ənd 'ɑːftər aiv biːn ˈskript

Stuart and Graham

Stuart   Did you manage to finish that film-script in good time?

Graham   Oh yes, in fact I finished it on the tenth of October, with almost three weeks to spare.

Stuart   That was splendid. When we last talked about it you thought that it probably couldn't be done in less than six months.

Graham   That's quite right, and at times it almost drove me crazy. But Chris helped me tremendously. She typed the text and kept the flat quiet, took the kids out for walks and so on, and brought cups of coffee or glasses of squash at the appropriate times. And food, too, of course. I eat much more since I stopped smoking.

Stuart   You don't look as if you have a weight problem.

Graham   I didn't whilst I smoked, but then my waistline started to bulge quite distinctly and my clothes didn't fit me.

Stuart   Middle-aged spread, eh?

Graham   Exactly. And I couldn't afford to get new suits and things, so I decided to eat slightly less. That worked quite quickly.

Stuart   It certainly helps. But to get back to this film-script. Is it an original story or did you adapt somebody else's?

Graham   Oh, it's an adaptation of a thriller by Frank Strangelove, called *Lightning Always Strikes Twice*. Have you read Strangelove's stories at all?

Stuart   I don't think so. What's the subject?

Graham   It's about this chap who wants to kill his wealthy aunt, so he reconstructs an accident he once witnessed.

Stuart   And that's how the lightning strikes twice, I suppose.

Graham   Correct. In my view it's a stupid sort of plot, but you can't quarrel with your bread and butter, and I think I've managed to make most of the characters quite human.

Stuart   Great, but isn't it something of a waste for a chap with your talent to be tackling hack jobs like that?

Graham   The trouble is that I don't make much from my serious work, so script-writing pays the bills. I'm not one of those artists who thrives on starvation.

Stuart   No, but doesn't it take too much of your time? If you spend nine-tenths of your life on films, there isn't much left for your novels and poems.

Graham   Oh, it's not nine-tenths, not more than half. So I've plenty of time for my other stuff. Besides, it makes a change; I quite enjoy it, mostly. Then when I've finished I can get back to my novels feeling refreshed and strengthened.

Stuart   You don't keep both going?

Graham   No, I find that practically impossible. It seems as though one kind of writing obstructs the other, and after I've been script-writing

raitiŋ fər ə ˌwail| it ˌteiks miː 'kwait 'sʌm ˇtaim| tə 'set| 'bæk tə mai ˋsiəriəs ˌstʌf‖

ˋstjuːət   'wɔt ˋleŋkθ əv ˌtaim‖ ˌdeiz| ˌwiːks| ˌmʌnθs‖

ˋgreiəm   ˋnou| 'nɔt ˇmʌnθs‖ ˇjuːʒ|i| its ə ˌkweʃtʃən əv 'ten ɔː 'twelv ˋdeiz‖ ai 'hæf tə 'θrou əˇwei| ˌpræktikli 'evriθiŋ ai ˋrait tə bi ˌgin wið‖ bət 'grædʒəli it 'kʌmz ˋbæk‖ ənd 'ɑːftər ə 'kʌp| əv ˇwiːks| 'θiŋz get ˋbetə‖

ˋstjuːət   juː 'dount 'stɔp ˌraitiŋ fə ·ðæt ·taim‖

ˋgreiəm   ˋnou| 'ðæt 'dʌzn̩t ˋwəːk‖ aiv 'gɔt tə 'kiːp ˋstrʌgliŋ| it 'wount kʌm 'bæk wið'aut ˋswet‖ biˋsaidz| it ə'fendz mai 'diːpist ˋinstiŋkts ˌnɔt tə ˌrait‖

ˋstjuːət   juː 'rait 'evri ˋdei| ˌduː juː‖

ˋgreiəm   ˋjes| ik'sept fər ə 'kʌp| əv ˋwiːks 'breik in ˇsʌmə‖ in ˋmoust riˌspekts| its 'laik ˋʌðə piːp|z ˌdʒɔbz‖ it di'mɑːndz regjəˋlærəti| ənd 'priti 'strikt ˋdisiplin‖ its 'feit|i ˇiːzi| tə 'faind ik'skjuːsiz fə ˋnɔt ˌraitiŋ‖ bət ðə prəˇfeʃn̩‖ 'kɑːnt ə'fɔːd tə 'let imself bi diˋstræktid‖

ˋstjuːət   it 'mʌst ri'kwaiə 'greit 'streŋkθ əv ˋmaind ˌsʌmtaimz‖

ˋgreiəm   ət ˇfəːst‖ bət 'wen ðə 'hæbits ˇfɔːmd| it bi'kʌmz inˋstiŋktiv‖

ˋstjuːət   ai 'mʌsn̩t di'strækt juː eni ˋmɔː‖ ail 'kɔːl 'raund 'nekst ˋwiːk əˌbaut ˌðouz ˌʃelvz‖

ˋgreiəm   ˋθæŋks‖ 'gud ˌbai‖

for a while it takes me quite some time to settle back to my serious stuff.

Stuart   What length of time? Days, weeks, months?

Graham   No, not months. Usually, it's a question of ten or twelve days. I have to throw away practically everything I write to begin with, but gradually it comes back and after a couple of weeks things get better.

Stuart   You don't stop writing for that time?

Graham   No, that doesn't work. I've got to keep struggling. It won't come back without sweat. Besides, it offends my deepest instincts not to write.

Stuart   You write every day, do you?

Graham   Yes, except for a couple of weeks break in summer. In most respects it's like other people's jobs; it demands regularity and pretty strict discipline. It's fatally easy to find excuses for not writing, but the professional can't afford to let himself be distracted.

Stuart   It must require great strength of mind sometimes.

Graham   At first. But when the habit's formed it becomes instinctive.

Stuart   I mustn't distract you any more. I'll call round next week about those shelves.

Graham   Thanks. Goodbye.

igˈzɑːmp|z	ˈfiːl	ˈfil	ˈfel	ˈsiːt	ˈsit	ˈset
	ˈbiːn	ˈbin	ˈben	ˈsiːks	ˈsiks	ˈseks
	ˈliːd	ˈlid	ˈled	ˈriːtʃiz	ˈritʃiz	ˈretʃiz

ˈdʒimi ən ˈben

ˈben ˈθriliŋ| ˈiznt it ‖

ˈdʒimi ˈðis ˈpiktʃə juː ˌmiːn‖ ˈjes| it ˈiz‖ hiː ˈsiːmz tuː əv ˈtriːtid ðə ˈsiː laik ə ˈliviŋ ˈkriːtʃə‖ ən ðə ˈliviŋ ˌfigəz| ˈðiːz ˈpiːp| ɔn ðə ˇbiːtʃ fər ˌinstəns| ən ðə ˈʃiːp ɔn ðə ˇhilz| ˈsimpli əz ˈdekərətiv ˇθiŋz| əz ˈded əz ðə ˈpeb|z| ɔː ðə ˈʃelz‖

ˈben ai əˈgriː| its iŋˈkredəb|‖ aiv ˈnevə ˈsiːn ˈeniθiŋ əv ˌhiz| ðəts imˈprest miː ˈhɑːf sou ˌdiːpli əz ˌðis‖ hiː ˈtendz tə biː ə ˈbit ækəˈdemik ˌdʒenrəli‖

ˈdʒimi ˈhuː ˈiz iː‖ ðə ˈsignətʃə ˈdʌznt ˈmiːn eniθiŋ tə ˌmiː‖

ˈben ˈou| its ˈpiːtə ˈkeni‖ ˈðis iz iz ˈsekənd eksiˌbiʃn| ənd its ˈinfinətli ˈbetə ðən iz ˇpriːviəs wʌn‖

ˈdʒimi it ˈsiːmz ˈpriti imˈpresiv tə ˇmiː‖ ai ˈget ði: imˇpreʃn| ðət iːz əbˈsest bai ðə ˈsiː‖ ət ˈliːst ˈtwenti əv ˌðiːz ˌpiktʃəz ˌdiːl wið it‖

ˈben ˈwel| hiː ˈlivz in ˈhedbi| ə ˈlit| ˈfiʃiŋ vilidʒ in ˈdevn‖ sou hiːz ˈveri ˈintimətli kənˈsəːnd wið ðə ˌsiː| ən its iˈfekt ɔn ðə ˈpiːp| iː ˈlivz wið‖ ˈæz juː ˈsed ə ˈminit əˇgou| hiː ˈsiːz it əz ə ˈliviŋ indiˈvidjuəl‖ ˈviʃəs ən ˈdʒent|‖ ˈbitər ən ˈswiːt‖ ˈdʒenərəs əz ə ˇfrend| bət ˈterəb| əz ən ˈenəmi‖

ˈdʒimi ˈhæv juː ˈevə ˌmet im‖ ai ˈget ði: imˌpreʃn| əv ə ˈveri ˈdiːp ˈsimpəθi biˌtwiːn ˌjuː ən ˌhim‖

ˈben ˈjes| ðəər ˈiz‖ ai ˈmet im əˇridʒinəli| in ˈvenis| in ˈnaintiːn ˈfifti ˈsevn| ən wiːv ˈbiːn ˈfrendz ˈevə ˈsins‖ wiː ˈmiːt ˈpriti ˈregjələli‖ ai ˈgiv im ə ˈbed wenˌevər iːz in ˌðis viˌsinəti| ən ai ˈfriːkwəntli ˈvizit im in ˈhedbi‖

ˈdʒimi ai ˈsiː‖ hau ˈveri ˈintrəstiŋ‖ də juː ˈθiŋk ˌai kud ·miːt im‖

ˈben its ə ˈbit ˈdifək|t ət ˌpreznt| hiːz in ˈitəli til ˌiːstə‖ bət ˈgiv miː jɔːr əˇdres| ən wiːl ˈfiks ə ˈmiːtiŋ wen iːz in ˈiŋglənd əˌgen‖

Examples

feel	fill	fell	seat	sit	set
bean	bin	Ben	seeks	six	sex
lead	lid	led	reaches	riches	wretches

Jimmy and Ben

Ben Thrilling, isn't it?

Jimmy This picture, you mean. Yes, it is. He seems to have treated the sea like a living creature, and the living figures – these people on the beach, for instance, and the sheep on the hills – simply as decorative things, as dead as the pebbles or the shells.

Ben I agree, it's incredible. I've never seen anything of his that's impressed me half so deeply as this. He tends to be a bit academic, generally.

Jimmy Who is he? The signature doesn't mean anything to me.

Ben Oh, it's Peter Kenny. This is his second exhibition and it's infinitely better than his previous one.

Jimmy It seems pretty impressive to me. I get the feeling that he's obsessed by the sea. At least twenty of these pictures deal with it.

Ben Well, he lives in Headby, a little fishing village in Devon, so he's very intimately concerned with the sea and its effect on the people he lives with. As you said a minute ago, he sees it as a living individual, vicious and gentle, bitter and sweet, generous as a friend but terrible as an enemy.

Jimmy Have you ever met him? I get the impression of a very deep sympathy between you and him.

Ben Yes, there is. I met him originally in Venice in 1957, and we've been friends ever since. We meet pretty regularly; I give him a bed whenever he's in this vicinity, and I frequently visit him in Headby.

Jimmy I see. How very interesting. Do you think I could meet him?

Ben It's a bit difficult at present. He's in Italy till Easter. But give me your address and we'll fix a meeting when he's in England again.

ig'zɑːmp|z   'pen 'pæn 'pʌn   'bet 'bæt 'bʌt
              'bed 'bæd 'bʌd   'meʃ 'mæʃ 'mʌʃ
              'hel 'hæl 'hʌl   'seks 'sæks 'sʌks

'dæd ən 'ted

'ted   'hevn̩z ˌdæd| 'let miː 'help‖ juːl 'end ʌp wið 'bæk trʌb| əˌgen| if
 juː ˌkæri ˌðæt eni ˌfəːðə‖ it 'mʌst 'wei ə 'tʌn‖
'dæd   'jes| its 'hevi iˇnʌf| ai kənˇfes‖ ail 'dʒʌst 'rest it ɔn ðæt 'elm stʌmp|
if juːl ˌlend ə ˌhænd ·sʌn‖ 'ðen pəˌhæps| it wud biː 'betə tə 'get ðə
'bærou‖ its ə 'dev| tə ˌkæri‖ 'fetʃ ðə 'blæk ˌbærou| ðiː 'ʌðə wʌn
hæz ə 'krækt 'hænd|‖
'ted   'kæn wiː 'get ðə 'bærou 'rait 'ʌp tə ðə ˌstʌmp‖ it | bi 'mʌtʃ 'les
'trʌb| if wiː ˌkæn‖
'dæd   'jes| 'ðæts 'wʌndəf|‖ 'ʌp it ˌkʌmz‖ 'bæk 'ðæt 'wei 'dʒʌst ə
ˌfrækʃn̩‖ 'splendid‖ 'wel 'dʌn ˌted‖ aim 'glæd juː ˌhæpənd tə ˌkʌm
ˌʌp ˌdʒʌs ˌðen‖ aid 'nevər əv ˌmænidʒd it ˌsiŋg| ˌhændid‖ its 'mʌtʃ
'heviə ðən ai iˇmædʒind‖
'ted   'iz it 'sʌmθiŋ ˌspeʃ|‖
'dæd   'jes| its ə 'prezn̩t fə jɔː 'mʌðə‖ its auə 'twentiəθ 'wediŋ ænivəːsri
ˌneks ˌmʌndi| ənd ai wəz 'lʌki i'nʌf tə 'kʌm əkrɔs 'sʌmθiŋ 'æbsəluːtli
'stʌniŋ‖ its ə 'desk‖
'ted   bət 'mʌm 'hæz ə ˌdesk‖
'dæd   'ou 'jes| bət 'ðæts ðə 'wʌn wiː 'hæd wen wiː wə 'mærid‖ it wəz
'sekənd 'hænd 'ðen| ən ʃiː 'nevə 'lʌvd it ˌveri ˌmʌtʃ‖ bət 'ðis wʌnz|
fænˇtæstik‖ 'æbsəluːtli 'lʌvli‖
'ted   'sʌtʃ inˇθuːziæzm̩ ˌdæd‖ bət wiː 'mʌs 'get it 'ʌndə 'kʌvə| ai 'dount
ig'zæktli 'trʌst ðə 'weðə‖ 'ʃæl wiː 'rʌn it tə ðə ˌfrʌnt ·dɔːr| ɔː ðə
'bæk‖
'dæd   'nou| jɔː 'mʌðə 'mʌsn̩t 'hæv it til 'mʌndi‖ wiːl 'stænd it in ðə
'hʌt ət ðə 'bæk əv ðə 'gærɑːʒ| ən 'kʌvər it wið 'sækiŋ‖ jɔː 'mʌðər
| 'nevə ˌluk ʌndə ˌðæt‖ 'hʌri ˌʌp| ʃiːl bi 'kʌmiŋ 'bæk ˌprezn̩tli‖
'ted   ðə 'hʌt 'dʌzn̩t 'liːk| ˌdʌz it‖ it wud bi 'bæd 'lʌk if ðə 'desk wəz
ˇdæmidʒd‖
'dæd   'bæd 'lʌk‖ it wud bi 'trædʒik‖ bət ðə 'hʌts 'nevə biːn ˌdæmp‖
'kʌm ˌɔn‖

Examples

pen	pan	pun	bet	bat	but
bed	bad	bud	mesh	mash	mush
hell	Hal	hull	sex	sacks	sucks

Dad and Ted

Ted Heavens, Dad, let me help. You'll end up with back trouble again if you carry that any further. It must weigh a ton.

Dad Yes, it's heavy enough, I confess. I'll just rest it on that elm-stump, if you'll lend a hand, son. Then perhaps it would be better to get the barrow; it's a devil to carry. Fetch the black barrow, the other one has a cracked handle.

Ted Can we get the barrow right up to the stump? It'll be much less trouble if we can.

Dad Yes, that's wonderful. Up it comes. Back that way just a fraction. Splendid! Well done, Ted. I'm glad you happened to come up just then. I'd never have managed it single-handed. It's much heavier than I imagined.

Ted Is it something special?

Dad Yes, it's a present for your mother. It's our twentieth wedding anniversary next Monday, and I was lucky enough to come across something absolutely stunning. It's a desk.

Ted But Mum has a desk.

Dad Oh, yes, but that's the one we had when we were married. It was second-hand then, and she never loved it very much. But this one's fantastic. Absolutely lovely.

Ted Such enthusiasm, Dad. But we must get it under cover; I don't exactly trust the weather. Shall we run it to the front door or the back?

Dad No, your mother mustn't have it till Monday. We'll stand it in the hut at the back of the garage and cover it with sacking. Your mother will never look under that. Hurry up, she'll be coming back presently.

Ted The hut doesn't leak, does it? It would be bad luck if the desk was damaged.

Dad Bad luck! It would be tragic. But the hut's never been damp. Come on.

ig'zɑːmp|z   'lʌk   'lɑːk   'lɔk   'kʌp   'kɑːp   'kɔp
                'bʌks   'bɑːks   'bɔks   'kʌd   'kɑːd   'kɔd
                'lʌst   'lɑːst   'lɔst   'dʌn   'dɑːn   'dɔn

'sɑːndrə ən 'dʒɒn

'sɑːndrə   'dʒɒn| θæŋk 'gɔd juːv 'kʌm ət 'lɑːst|| ðə 'kɑːz ˌgɒn||

'dʒɒn   'nɒnsəns| it 'kɑːnt əv ˌgɒn|| juː 'mʌst əv fə'gɒtn̩ wɛər it 'wɒz||

'sɑːndrə   'nou| 'ɔnisli|| 'ɑːftə ai 'drɔpt ˇjuː| ai 'pɑːkt it 'ɔpəzit ðə 'bʌs
            stɔp| ən 'pɔpt 'intə ði: ɔp'tiʃn̩z| ən 'gɔt mai 'glɑːsiz|| ai 'wɔznt ˇlɔŋ||
            it wəz 'dʒʌst ɔn 'wʌn ə'klɔk| ən ðə 'ʃɔps wə ˌdʒʌʃ ˌʃʌtiŋ| ənd ai
            'wɒntid ə 'kɑːd| fə 'mɑːθə||

'dʒɒn   sou 'ɑːftə juː 'gɔt 'mɑːθəz ˇkɑːd| juː 'hʌrid 'ɔf tə ðə 'kɑː:||

'sɑːndrə   'nɒt ət ˇwʌns|| ai wəz 'dʒʌs 'pɑːsiŋ 'tɔmsn̩z| ənd ai 'sʌdn̩li gɔt
            'wʌrid əbaut 'fɑːðəz 'klɔk| ən 'rʌʃt ˌɔf| tuː 'ɑːsk ðəm wɔt 'tʃɑːns
            ðɛə 'wɔz əv 'hʌriːiŋ it ʌp|| 'mʌðəz 'stɑːtiŋ tə ˇfʌs əˌbaut it||

'dʒɒn   'hæd juː ˌlɔkt ðə ·kɑː:||

'sɑːndrə   ai 'kɑːnt əv ˌdʌn|| ai 'mʌst əv fə'gɒtn̩| bikɔz ðə 'kɑː ˇkiːz| 'nɒt
            in mai 'ʃɔpiŋ ˌbɑːskit||

'dʒɒn   sou it wəz 'ʌn'lɔkt|| 'eniwʌn kud əv ˌstɑːtid it ˌʌp| ən 'gɒn 'ɔf
            wið it|| 'dɑːliŋ| 'juː 'ɑːr ə ˌklɔt| 'ɑːnt juː|| juː 'mʌs 'pɑːk ðə 'kɑːr in
            ðə 'kɑː ˌpɑːk|| ənd juː 'mʌst 'lɔk it|| 'hau 'lɔŋ wə juː 'gɒn||

'sɑːndrə   'nɒt ˇlɔŋ|| 'tɔmsn̩z wə 'ʃʌt| ənd aid gɔt 'hɑːf'wei tə ðə ˌkɑː:|
            wen 'mɒli 'kɑːtə ˌstɔpt miː|| ʃiː 'wɒntid tə di'skʌs ðə 'drɑːmə ˌklʌb||

'dʒɒn   sou 'wen ət 'lɑːst juː 'gɔt aut əv 'mɒli 'kɑːtəz ˌklʌtʃiz| juː 'trɔtid
            'ɔf tə ðə 'kɑː:||

'sɑːndrə   'jes| ən 'ðɛər it 'wɒz 'gɒn| 'lɔst||

'dʒɒn   ˇgɒn| bət 'nɒt 'lɔst ˌlʌv||

'sɑːndrə   ˌwɒt||

'dʒɒn   'ɑːftə juː 'drɔpt miː ˌɔf| ai 'riəlaizd ðət aid fə'gɒtn̩ mai 'wɒlit| ən
            ðət it 'mʌs biː in ðə 'kɑː:|| juːd ˇpɑːkt it| ən 'gɒn| wen ˌai ˌgɔt ·ðɛə||
            sou ai dʒʌs 'drouv it tə ðə ˌkɑː ·pɑːk| ˌlɔkt it| ənd 'hʌŋ ə'baut||

'sɑːndrə   jɔː 'hɔrəbl̩||| it wəz 'sʌtʃ ə 'ʃɔk||

'dʒɒn   'kʌm ən hæv ə 'kʌp əv 'kɔfi| ən 'stɔp 'fʌsiŋ|| ən 'lɔk ðə 'kɑːr
            əˌnʌðə ·taim||

Examples	luck	lark	lock	cup	carp	cop
	bucks	barks	box	cud	card	cod
	lust	last	lost	done	darn	Don

Sandra and John

Sandra John! Thank God you've come at last. The car's gone.

John Nonsense, it can't have gone. You must have forgotten where it was.

Sandra No, honestly, after I dropped you I parked it opposite the bus stop and popped into the optician's and got my glasses. I wasn't long, it was just on one o'clock and the shops were just shutting, and I wanted a card for Martha.

John So after you'd got Martha's card, you hurried off to the car.

Sandra Not at once; I was just passing Thomson's and I suddenly got worried about father's clock and rushed off to ask them what chance there was of hurrying it up. Mother's starting to fuss about it.

John Had you locked the car?

Sandra I can't have done, I must have forgotten, because the car key's not in my shopping basket.

John So it was unlocked. Anyone could have started it up and gone off with it. Darling, you are a clot, aren't you? You must park the car in the car-park and you must lock it. How long were you gone?

Sandra Not long. Thomson's were shut, and I'd got halfway to the car when Molly Carter stopped me. She wanted to discuss the drama club.

John So when at last you got out of Molly Carter's clutches you trotted off to the car.

Sandra Yes, and there it was gone, lost.

John Gone, but not lost, love.

Sandra What?

John After you dropped me off I realised I'd forgotten my wallet and that it must be in the car. You'd parked it and gone when I got there, so I just drove it to the car-park, locked it and hung about.

Sandra You're horrible! It was such a shock!

John Come and have a cup of coffee and stop fussing. And lock the car another time.

igˈzɑːmpǀz   ˈkɔd   ˈkɔːd   ˈkoud   ˈkɔt   ˈkɔːt   ˈkout
             ˈpɔl   ˈpɔːl   ˈpoul   ˈkɔst   ˈkɔːst   ˈkoust
             ˈʃɔn   ˈʃɔːn   ˈʃoun   ˈstɔk   ˈstɔːk   ˈstouk

                        ˈpɔːliːn ən ˈdʒɔn

ˈpɔːliːn   ðɛəz ə ˈfoun kɔːl ˌfɔː juːǀ ˈdʒou ˈwɔːnəǁ
ˈdʒɔn   ˈou ˈnou ˌpɔːliːnǀ ai ˈdount ˈwɔnt tə ˌtɔːk tə ˌdʒou ət ðə ˌmouməntǁ
         ˈsei aim ˈnɔt ət ˈhoumǁ
ˈpɔːliːn   ˇsɔriǀ aiv ɔːlˈredi ˈtould im aid ˈkɔːl juːǁ
ˈdʒɔn   ou ˈɔːlˌraitǁ ˌdʒouǁ . . . ˈnouǀ ˈnɔt əˈtɔːlǀ juː ˈnou aim ɔːlwiz ət
         ˌjɔː diˈspouzǀǁ ˈwɔt ˈwɔz it juː ˈwɔntidǁ . . . ðə ˈlɔːnˌmouəǁ ˈnouǀ
         ˈnɔt ət ðə ˇmouməntǁ ai ˈmoud ðə ˈlɔːn ðis ˈmɔːniŋ . . . əf ˈkɔːs juː
         kən ˌbɔrou itǀ bət ˈwɔts ˈrɔŋ wið ˈjɔːz . . . ˈou ˈlɔːdǀ ˈwɔt ə ˈbɔːǀ
         it ǀ ˈkɔst ə ˈfɔːtʃənǁ ou ˇdʒouǀ juː ˈnou its ˈnɔt ə ˈmoutəˌmouəǀ laik
         ˇjɔːzǀ ˈdount juːǁ . . . ai ˈθɔːt aid ˈbetə ˈwɔːn juː ˌðouǁ . . . ai ˈnou ai
         ˌɔːtǀ bət its ðə ˈkɔstǁ ai ˈkudn̩t əˈfɔːd bouθ ə ˈhɔlədi in ˈkɔːnwɔːl ˈænd
         ə ˌmoutəˌmouəǁ . . . də juː ˈwɔnt mi tə trænsˈpɔːt it əˈkrɔs ðə ˌroud
         fɔː juːǁ . . . ai ˈθɔːt ˌsouǁ ˈhould ˌɔn ðenǀ ai ˈwount bi ˌlɔŋǁ
ˈpɔːliːn   sou iː ˈwɔnts ə ˈloun ə ðə ˈmouəǁ
ˈdʒɔn   juː ˌnou aim ˈɔːfli ˈfɔnd əv ˌdʒouǀ bət ðɛər ˈɔːt tə biː ə ˈlɔːǀ əgenst
         ˈɔːl ðə ˈbɔrouiŋ iː ˌgouz ˌin fɔːǁ ˈounli ə ˈfɔːtnait əˌgouǀ it wəz ðə
         ˈsɔːǁ
ˈpɔːliːn   ən biˈfɔː ˇðætǀ hiː ˈgɔt ˈhould əv jɔː ˈblouˌtɔːtʃǁ ən ˈwɔt wil it
         ˈbiː təˈmɔrouǁ ˈmai ˈklouzˌhɔːsǀ ɔː ˈjɔː ˈboutǀ ɔː ˈgɔd nouz ˈwɔtǁ
ˈdʒɔn   ˈdount bi ˌkrɔsǁ its ˈounli biˈkɔz iːz ˈɔn iz ˈoun juː ˌnouǁ hiːz
         ˈlounliǁ ən ˇbɔrouiŋǀ ˌgivz im ə ˈsɔːt əv ˈsouʃǀ ˈkɔntæktǁ
ˈpɔːliːn   ai ˈspouz ˈsouǁ ˈɔf juː ˌgou ðenǀ ˈteik ðə ˌmouərǀ ənd ˈhæv ə
         ˌtɔːk tə ðə ·pɔːr ould ·soulǁ bət ˈdount bi ˈlɔŋǀ ɔːr iːl ˈbɔrou jɔːr
         ˈaibɔːlzǁ

Examples	cod	cord	code	cot	caught	coat
	Poll	Paul	pole	cost	coursed	coast
	shone	shorn	shown	stock	stalk	stoke

Pauline and John

Pauline　There's a phone-call for you. Joe Warner.

John　Oh, no, Pauline. I don't want to talk to Joe at the moment. Say I'm not at home.

Pauline　Sorry, I've already told him I'd call you.

John　Oh, alright. Joe?... No, not at all. You know I'm always at your disposal. What was it you wanted?... The lawn-mower? No, not at the moment, I mowed the lawn this morning... Of course you can borrow it, but what's wrong with yours?... Oh, lord, what a bore! It'll cost a fortune. Oh, Joe, you know it's not a motor-mower like yours, don't you?... I thought I'd better warn you, though... I know I ought, but it's the cost; I couldn't afford both a holiday in Cornwall and a motor-mower... Do you want me to transport it across the road for you?... I thought so. Hold on, then. I won't be long.

Pauline　So he wants a loan of the mower.

John　You know, I'm awfully fond of Joe, but there ought to be a law against all the borrowing he goes in for. Only a fortnight ago it was the saw.

Pauline　And before that he got hold of your blow-torch. And what will it be tomorrow? My clothes horse or your boat, or God knows what.

John　Don't be cross. It's only because he's on his own, you know. He's lonely, and borrowing gives him a sort of social contact.

Pauline　I suppose so. Off you go, then, take the mower and have a talk to the poor old soul. But don't be long or he'll borrow your eyeballs.

igˈzaːmplz	ˈpul	ˈpuːl	ˈpuli	ˈpuəli	ˈʃuː	ˈʃuə
	ˈsut	ˈsuːt	ˈgud	ˈguəd	ˈstjuːd	ˈstjuəd

'mjuəriəl ən ˋhjuː

ˋmjuəriəl 'kud juː 'get mai ˏkukəri ·buk| frəm ðə ˏbaːθrum||

ˋhjuː ðə ˏbaːθrum|| ˋðæts ə ˌkjuəriəs ˌpleis fər ə ˏkukəri ·buk||

ˋmjuəriəl ai 'juːʒḷi 'plæn ðə ˋkukiŋ in ðə ˏbaːθ|| its ˋsuːðiŋ| ənd it 'puts miː in ə 'gud 'muːd fə ðiː 'æktʃuəl ˋkukiŋ||

ˋhjuː 'gud fə ˋjuː|| 'wɔt əv juː biːn 'duːiŋ 'djuəriŋ ðə ˋdei||

ˋmjuəriəl 'pjuə ruːˋtiːn|| ai 'did ə 'tuər əv ðə ˏʃɔps|| 'lukt 'in ət ðə ˏdʒuələz| ən gɔt ə 'bjuːtəfḷ ˇspuːn| fə ðə 'muəz 'njuː ˇbeibi|| ən səm 'bluː ˋwul| fə jɔː 'njuː ˋpulouvə||

ˋhjuː 'nɔt ət ðə ˇdʒuələz| ˋʃuəli||

ˋmjuəriəl ət ðə ˋwul ʃɔp juː ˌguːs|| ai 'peid ðə ˏfjuəl ·bil| ən ðiː inˏʃuərəns| ən 'gɔt səm 'fuːd fə ˋpusi|| ai 'lukt ət səm ˋʃuːz| in ˋfuləz| ˋtuː|| bət ai 'kudn̩t siː 'eniθiŋ ðət wud ˋsuːt mi||

ˋhjuː ˏkudn̩t juː||

ˋmjuəriəl ˋnou| ðei wər 'aiðə 'tuː diˋmjuə ˏlukiŋ| ɔː 'tuː 'luːs in ðə ˋfut||

ˋhjuː ai 'wudn̩t 'laik juː 'lukiŋ 'aiðə diˇmjuər| 'ɔː ˋluːs||

ˋmjuəriəl aim 'ʃuə juː ˋwud juː ˏwulf|| ˋou| 'ðen ðɛə wəz ðə ˋbutʃəz|| ai wəz ˋfjuəriəs||

ˋhjuː 'fjuəriəs wið ðə ˏbutʃə| 'mistə ˏbul|| hiːz 'veri ˋgud tə juː əz ə ˏruːl||

ˋmjuəriəl nou 'nɔt wið 'mistə ˇbul|| wið ðis 'stjuːpid ˋwumən||

ˋhjuː ˋwɔt ˌstjuːpid ˌwumən||

ˋmjuəriəl wel ðə 'ʃɔp wəz ˋfulə ðən ˏjuːʒuəl| sou ai 'tuk mai 'pleis in ðə ˇkjuː| ən ðis 'luːnətik əv ə ˏwumən| 'puʃt ˏθruː|| 'stud ɔn mai ˋfut| ˋtuː|| ənd ri'fjuːzd tə ˋkjuː|| 'pjuə ˋruːdnəs|| bət 'mistə 'bul wəz 'æbsəluːtli sjuːˋpəːb|| hiː tuk 'wʌn ˇluk æt əː| ən ˌbuːmd 'misiz ˋguəli|| ai əˇʃuə juː| ðət ðə 'suːnə juː 'dʒɔin ðə ˇkjuː| ðə 'suːnə juː wil bi ˋsəːvd|| ˋθæŋk ju||

ˋhjuː ˋðæt ʃud ˌkjuə həːr əv ˏkjuː·dʒʌmpiŋ||

ˋmjuəriəl juː 'kaːnt 'kjuə ðiː iŋˇkjuərəbḷ||

Examples	pull	pool	pulley	poorly	shoe	sure
	soot	suit	good	gourd	stewed	steward

Muriel and Hugh

Muriel   Could you get my cookery book from the bathroom?

Hugh   The bathroom? That's a curious place for a cookery book.

Muriel   I usually plan the cooking in the bath. It's soothing, and it puts me in a good mood for the actual cooking.

Hugh   Good for you. What have you been doing during the day?

Muriel   Pure routine. I did a tour of the shops; looked in at the jeweller's and got a beautiful spoon for the Moores' new baby, and some blue wool for your new pullover.

Hugh   Not at the jeweller's, surely?

Muriel   At the wool shop, you goose. I paid the fuel bill and the insurance, and got some food for Pussy. I looked at some shoes in Fuller's, too, but I couldn't see anything that would suit me.

Hugh   Couldn't you?

Muriel   No, they were either too demure-looking or too loose in the foot.

Hugh   I wouldn't like you looking either demure or loose.

Muriel   I'm sure you would, you wolf. Oh, then there was the butcher's. I was furious.

Hugh   Furious with the butcher? Mr Bull? He's very good to you as a rule.

Muriel   No, not with Mr Bull. With this stupid woman.

Hugh   What stupid woman?

Muriel   Well, the shop was fuller than usual, so I took my place in the queue, and this lunatic of a woman pushed through – stood on my foot, too – and refused to queue. Pure rudeness. But Mr Bull was absolutely superb. He took one look at her and boomed: 'Mrs Gourley, I assure you that the sooner you join the queue the sooner you will be served. Thank you.'

Hugh   That should cure her of queue-jumping.

Muriel   You can't cure the incurable.

ig'zaːmp|z   'həːd   'haːd   'pəːs   'paːs   'fɔːwəd 'fɔːwəːd
              'bəːn   'baːn   'pəːtʃt   'paːtʃt   'feiməs 'kɔməːs
              'fəːm   'faːm   'ləːks   'laːks

'bəːnəd 'həːli ən 'tʃaːlz 'təːnə

'tʃaːlz gud 'aːftə'nuːn mistə ˌhəːli| 'aim 'tʃaːlz 'təːnə| ðə 'pəːsə'nel
  diˌrektər əv ˌkaːvər ən ˌfəːθ‖ juːv 'aːnsəd ən əd'vəːtismənt| tə 'wəːk
  in auə 'pəːtʃəsiŋ diˌpaːtmənt‖ 'tel mi 'fəːst əbaut 'fəːmz juːv 'wəːkt
  fɔːr in ðə ˌpaːst‖
'bəːnəd 'səːtn̩li sə‖ mai 'fəːs ˌdʒɔb| wəz wið ə bə'naːnə ˌməːtʃənt| in ðə
  'maːkit ət 'kɔvn̩t 'gaːdn̩‖ ai wəz 'pəːsnəl ə'sistənt tə ðə kə'məːʃ|
  ˌmænidʒə‖ it 'təːnd 'aut ðət ðɛə wəz 'nou 'tʃaːns əv 'fəːðər
  əd'vaːnsmənt| sou 'aːftər ə 'jəːr| ai træns'fəːd tə ðə sə'bəːbən
  di'veləpmənt ˌkʌmpəni| 'hiər in 'bəːmiŋəm| ðə 'fəːm ai 'wəːk fɔː
  'nau‖
'tʃaːlz juː wər ət 'juːni'vəːsəti in ˌbəːmiŋəm| ˌwəːnt juː‖
'bəːnəd 'jes sər| in ðə 'dʒəːmən diˌpaːtmənt‖ ai 'paːst wið ə 'fəːs 'klaːs|
  ən ðə prə'fesər 'aːst mi tə ri'təːn| əz hiz ri'səːtʃ əˌsistənt‖
'tʃaːlz wið ə 'tʃaːns əv 'dʒɔiniŋ ðə 'pəːmənənt 'staːf‖
'bəːnəd 'jes sə| bət ai 'təːnd it 'daun‖ ai pri'fəːd tə 'tʃaːns mai 'aːm in
  ðə kə'məːʃ| wəːld‖
'tʃaːlz ən jɔː 'səːtn̩| ˌaː juː| ðət jɔː 'haːts in 'kɔməːs‖
'bəːnəd 'pəːfiktli ˌsəːtn sə‖
'tʃaːlz ən 'wai də juː 'wɔnt tə 'kʌm tə 'kaːvər ən 'fəːθ in pəˌtikjələ‖
'bəːnəd bikəz aiv 'həːd frəm mai 'faːðə| ðət jɔːr ə 'maːvələs 'fəːm tə
  'wəːk fɔː‖
'tʃaːlz jɔː 'faːðə‖ juː 'aːnt bai 'eni 'tʃaːns 'həːbət ˌhəːliz ˌsʌn| ˌaː juː‖
'bəːnəd 'jes sə‖
'tʃaːlz əv 'həːli ən ˌbaːnz| 'in ˌkænədə‖
'bəːnəd 'jes sər| 'ɔtəwə‖ bət mai 'faːðə 'left ðə ˌfəːm| 'əːli 'laːst 'jəːr|
  ən ri'təːnd tuː 'iŋglənd‖ 'fəːs tə 'baːθ| ənd 'aːftəwədz tə 'bəːmiŋəm‖
'tʃaːlz jɔː 'faːðəz 'hiər in ˌbəːmiŋəm‖ ai 'hædn̩t 'həːd ə 'wəːd‖
'bəːnəd it wəz 'ounli 'laːst 'θəːzdi sə| ənd ai 'aːst im tə 'kiːp it 'daːk|
  til 'aːftə tə'dei‖
'tʃaːlz jɔː 'faːðər iz 'veri 'tʃaːmiŋ ən 'kəːtjəs mistə ˌhəːli‖ bət hiː wud
  'nevər ig'zəːt 'prefər| ɔn bi'haːf əv ən ˌʌndi'zəːviŋ 'pəːsn̩‖
'bəːnəd ai pri'fəːd 'nɔt tə 'tʃaːns it sə‖

Examples	heard	hard	purse	pass	forward	foreword
	burn	barn	perched	parched	famous	commerce
	firm	farm	lurks	larks		

Bernard Hurley and Charles Turner

Charles   Good afternoon, Mr Hurley. I'm Charles Turner, the personnel director of Carver and Firth. You've answered an advertisement to work in our purchasing department. Tell me first about firms you've worked for in the past.

Bernard   Certainly, sir. My first job was with a banana merchant in the market at Covent Garden. I was personal assistant to the commercial manager. It turned out that there was no chance of further advancement, so after a year I transferred to the Suburban Development Company here in Birmingham, the firm I work for now.

Charles   You were at university in Birmingham, weren't you?

Bernard   Yes, sir, in the German Department. I passed with a first-class, and the professor asked me to return as his research assistant.

Charles   With a chance of joining the permanent staff?

Bernard   Yes, sir, but I turned it down. I preferred to chance my arm in the commercial world.

Charles   And you're certain, are you, that your heart is in commerce?

Bernard   Perfectly certain, sir.

Charles   And why do you want to come to Carver and Firth in particular?

Bernard   Because I've heard from my father that you're a marvellous firm to work for.

Charles   Your father? You aren't by any chance Herbert Hurley's son, are you?

Bernard   Yes, sir.

Charles   Of Hurley and Barnes? In Canada?

Bernard   Yes, sir, Ottawa. But my father left the firm early last year and returned to England, first to Bath and afterwards to Birmingham.

Charles   Your father's here in Birmingham? I hadn't heard a word.

Bernard   It was only last Thursday, sir, and I asked him to keep it dark till after today.

Charles   Your father is very charming and courteous, Mr Hurley, but he would never exert pressure on behalf of an undeserving person.

Bernard   I preferred not to chance it, sir.

ig'zɑːmp|z   ˋbei   ˋbai   ˋbɔi   ˋpeiz   ˋpaiz   ˋpɔiz
          ˋlein   ˋlain   ˋlɔin   ˋpeint   ˋpaint   ˋpɔint
          ˋteil   ˋtail   ˋtɔil   ˋleitə   ˋlaitə   ˋlɔitə

'ailiːn ənd ˋrɔi

ˋrɔi   wɔt ə 'streindʒ ən 'fraitniŋ ˋnɔiz‖
ˋailiːn   ai 'laik ˋðæt‖ mai ˌvɔis wəz 'veri 'haili ˋpreizd əz ə ˌtʃaild‖
ˋrɔi   ən 'kwait ˋraitli ai ˌmei ˌsei‖ juː hæv ðə ˋvɔis əv ə ˋnaitiŋˌgeil mai ˌeindʒəl‖ 'wud juː 'laik səm ˌɔil fɔr it| in ðə 'ʃeip əv ə 'lait ˌeil‖
ˋailiːn   ˋrɔi| 'wai ə juː sou ˋbɔistrəs təˌnait‖
ˋrɔi   its ˋfraidi ˌlait əv mai ˌlaif| 'fraidi ˋnait| ə 'gei ən 'dʒɔiful ˋtaim‖ ðə 'tɔil əv ðə 'dei iz biˋhaind miː‖ ai həv iˋskeipt frəm mai 'pleis əv ˋvail imˋplɔimənt‖ 'dʒɔin miː in ə 'lait 'eil tə ˋselibreit it‖ let 'dʒɔi biː ˋʌnkənˋfaind‖
ˋailiːn   'dʒʌs 'trai ən ˋmɔdəreit jɔː ˌdʒɔi fər ə ˌwail‖ 'fraidi 'nait 'mei biː 'fain fə ˋjuː mai ˌbɔi| bət 'bɛər in ˇmaind| ðət 'dʒeik ən ˋdʒɔis | biː əˌraiviŋ in ə ˌbreis əv ˌʃeiks| ənd 'ai hæf tə 'beist ðə ˌdʒɔint| ˋbɔil ðə pəˌteitouz| 'meik ə ˌtraif‖ ən 'put səm ˋmeikʌp ɔn mai ˌfeis‖ ˋai dount iˌskeip frəm mai imˌplɔimənt ət ˌfaiv ɔn ˌfraidi‖
ˋrɔi   'sneiks əˋlaiv‖ 'dʒɔis ən ˋdʒeik‖ aiv 'left ðə 'wain ɔn ðə ˋtrein‖ it went 'rait 'aut əv mai ˋmaind‖
ˋailiːn   jɔːr ə 'fraitf‖ ˋlaiə ˌrɔi| jɔː ˌseiiŋ ðæt 'dʒʌs tuː əˋnɔi miː| ənd if ai 'get əˇnɔid| it ¦ ˌspɔil ðə 'houl əˋkeiʒn̩ ˌfɔː miː‖
ˋrɔi   ˋsɔri ˌailiːn‖ ˋnou| jɔː 'kwait ˇrait| aiv 'gɔt ðə 'wain in mai ˋkeis‖ ənd juːl biː 'haili diˋlaitid wið mai ˋtʃɔis| its jɔː ˋfeivrət‖
ˋailiːn   ʃæmˇpein‖ juː 'brait ˋbɔi‖
ˋrɔi   ˋwel| wiː 'ɑː 'seləbreitiŋ 'dʒɔisiz iŋˇgeidʒmənt‖ ənd wiː 'mait əz 'wel inˋdʒɔi it| ˋmaitn̩t wiː‖ ðæts ðə 'houl ˋpɔint‖
ˋailiːn   ˋai ʃ| in‚dʒɔi it| if ðɛəz ʃæmˇpein‖
ˋrɔi   'bai ðə ˋwei| ˋwɔts ðə ˋdʒɔint‖
ˋailiːn   ˋsəːlɔin‖
ˋrɔi   ˋmai ˌfeivrət‖ jɔːr ə 'greit ˋwaif‖ wel ail 'liːv juː 'tɔiliŋ ne 'mɔiliŋ ˌhiər| ən 'gou ənd 'lei ðə ˋteib‖
ˋailiːn   'nais aiˋdiə‖ ai 'dount 'kwait 'nou 'witʃ wei aim ˋpɔintiŋ sins ˌjuː ˙keim ˙in‖

Examples bay   by   boy   pays   pies   poise
          lane line loin   paint pint   point
          tale tile toil   later lighter loiter

Eileen and Roy

Roy What a strange and frightening noise!

Eileen I like that! My voice was very highly praised as a child.

Roy And quite rightly, I may say. You have the voice of a nightingale, my angel. Would you like some oil for it, in the shape of a light ale?

Eileen Roy, why are you so boisterous tonight?

Roy It's Friday, light of my life, Friday night! A gay and joyful time. The toil of the day is behind me; I have escaped from my place of vile employment. Join me in a light ale to celebrate it. Let joy be unconfined!

Eileen Just try and moderate your joy for a while. Friday night may be fine for you, my boy, but bear in mind that Joyce and Jake will be arriving in a brace of shakes, and I have to baste the joint, boil the potatoes, make a trifle, and put some make-up on my face. I don't escape from my employment at five on Friday.

Roy Snakes alive! Joyce and Jake! I've left the wine in the train. It went right out of my mind.

Eileen You're a frightful liar, Roy. You're saying that just to annoy me, and if I get annoyed it'll spoil the whole occasion for me.

Roy Sorry, Eileen. No, you're quite right, I've got the wine in my case and you'll be highly delighted with my choice. It's your favourite.

Eileen Champagne! You bright boy!

Roy Well, we are celebrating Joyce's engagement and we might as well enjoy it, mightn't we? That's the whole point.

Eileen I shall enjoy it if there's champagne.

Roy By the way, what's the joint?

Eileen Sirloin.

Roy My favourite! You're a great wife. Well, I'll leave you toiling and moiling here and go and lay the table.

Eileen Nice idea. I don't quite know which way I'm pointing since you came in.

ig'zɑːmp|z   ˈhau   ˈhou   ˈhuː   ˈfaul   ˈfoul   ˈfuːl
              ˈlaud   ˈloud   ˈluːd   ˈnaun   ˈnoun   ˈnuːn
              ˈrauz   ˈrouz   ˈruːz   əˈbaut   ə ˈbout   ə ˈbuːt

                ə ˈgoust in ðə ˌhaus

ˈdʒou   aiv 'faund ə ˈhaus| aiv 'faund ə ˈhaus‖

ˈdʒuːn   'dount 'ʃaut sou ˈlaud ˌdʒou| juːl 'weik ˈtouni‖ 'faund ə ˌhaus‖
       ˈou| ai 'duː 'houp its ˇtruː‖ 'wɛərəˈbauts‖

ˈdʒou   juː 'nou əz juː ə'proutʃ ðə ˌtaun| ðɛəz ðæt 'njuː ˌbaundri ·roud|
       ðət gouz 'raun ði: ˌautskəːts‖

ˈdʒuːn   'ai ˌnou| juː 'toul miː it wəz 'djuː tuː ˈoupən ˌsuːn‖

ˈdʒou   it ˈiz oupən| ˈnau‖ it wəz 'oupənd ɔn ˈtjuːzdi‖ ˈenihau| ai 'drouv
       'raund it fər ə'baut ə ˇmail| ən 'noutist ə 'lit| 'nærou ˇroud| gouiŋ
       'daun tuːˈɔːdz ðə ˈtaun‖ sou ai ˈfɔloud it| ən faund ðis 'ould ˈhaus|
       in its 'oun ˈgraundz‖

ˈdʒuːn   ən ˈould ˌhaus‖ ˈnɔt ˈtuː ould ai ˌhoup‖

ˈdʒou   'ou ˈnou| bət juː 'nou hau wiː 'louðd ðə ˈnjuː ˌhauziz ˌdaun ˌðɛə‖

ˈdʒuːn   ˈtruː‖ nau ˈtel miː əˌbaut it‖ 'hau meni ˈruːmz‖

ˈdʒou   ai 'kauntid ˈten‖ 'faiv ɔn ðə ˌgraund ·flɔːr| ən 'faiv ˈbedrumz‖
       ən səm 'juːsf| ˈauthauziz| 'raund ðə ˈbæk‖

ˈdʒuːn   it 'saundz ˈhjuːdʒ‖ ən 'nou 'daut ðə ˈprais wil biː ˌhjuːdʒ| ˈtuː‖

ˈdʒou   ˈnou| its əˈstaundiŋ‖ ˈθriː ˈθauzṇd ˈpaundz‖

ˈdʒuːn   ˈθriː ˈθauzṇd ˌpaundz‖ ˈðæts ə ˈluːdikrəs əˌmaunt if ðə ˌhaus iz
       ˌsaund‖ 'hau də juː 'nou it 'wount ˈfɔːl ˈdaun‖

ˈdʒou   it ˌwount ˌfɔːl ˌdaun| its ˌsaund i·nʌf‖ 'ou ˌwel| jɔː ˈbaund tə
       ˌfaind ˌaut ˌsuːnər ɔː ˌleitə| sou juː 'mei əz 'wel nou ˈnau‖ ðə 'prais
       iz sou ˇlou| ɔn ə'kaunt əv ðə ˈgoust‖

ˈdʒuːn   ðə ˇgoust‖ jɔː ˈdʒoukiŋ‖

ˈdʒou   ˈnou‖ ai 'faund ðə ˈpousmən ˌdʒʌs ˌdaun ðə ˌroud| ən ˈhiː ˌtould
       miː əˌbaut it‖ ðə ˈlouk|z siːm ˈpraud əv ðɛə ˌgoust‖

ˈdʒuːn   ˈdʒou ˈbraun| if 'juː sə'pouz fər ə ˇmoumənt| ðət 'aim 'muːviŋ
       intu: ə 'haus wið ə ˈgoust ˌprauliŋ əˌbaut it| jɔːr 'aut əv jɔː 'fuːliʃ
       ˈmaind‖

ˈdʒou   ˈou| ˈdʒuːn‖ juː ˌdount biˌliːv in ˌgousts‖

ˈdʒuːn   ˈnou| ai ˈdount‖ bət aiv ˈdʌn wiðaut 'gousts in ðə 'haus əntil
       ˇnau| ənd ai kən 'duː wiˈðaut ðəm in ðə ˈfjuːtʃə‖

Examples   how   hoe   who   foul   foal   fool
             loud   load   lewd   noun   known   noon
             rouse rose   ruse   about   a boat   a boot

A Ghost in the House

Joe   I've found a house! I've found a house!

June   Don't shout so loud, Joe. You'll wake Tony. Found a house? Oh, I do hope it's true. Whereabouts?

Joe   You know as you approach the town, there's that new boundary road that goes round the outskirts?

June   I know. You told me it was due to open soon.

Joe   It is open now. It was opened on Tuesday. Anyhow, I drove round it for about a mile, and noticed a little narrow road going down towards the town. So I followed it and found this old house, in its own grounds.

June   An old house? Not too old, I hope?

Joe   Oh, no, but you know how we loathed the new houses down there.

June   True. Now tell me about it. How many rooms?

Joe   I counted ten, five on the ground floor and five bedrooms. And some useful outhouses round the back.

June   It sounds huge. And no doubt the price will be huge, too.

Joe   No, it's astounding. Three thousand pounds.

June   Three thousand pounds? That's a ludicrous amount if the house is sound. How do you know it won't fall down?

Joe   It won't fall down, it's sound enough. Oh well, you're bound to find out sooner or later so you may as well know now. The price is so low on account of the ghost.

June   The ghost? You're joking.

Joe   No, I found the postman just down the road and he told me about it. The locals seem proud of their ghost.

June   Joe Brown, if you suppose for a moment that I'm moving into a house with a ghost prowling about it, you're out of your foolish mind.

Joe   Oh, June, you don't believe in ghosts.

June   No, I don't, but I've done without ghosts in the house until now, and I can do without them in the future.

ig'zɑ:mp|z   ˈʃeid   ˈʃed   ˈʃɛəd   ˈfeiz   ˈfez   ˈfɛəz
              ˋbeili   ˋbeli   ˋbɛəli   ˋkein   ˋken   ˋkɛən
              ˋbein   ˋben   ˋbɛən   ˋspeid   ˋsped   ˋspɛəd

'meivis ənd ˈʃɛərən

ˋmeivis   'wɛə wəz ðis ˈfoutəgrɑːf ˌteikən‖

ˈʃɛərən   it wəz 'teikən ət ˋbrɔːdstɛəz| wen wiː 'went ðɛə fər ə ˋdei‖ aiv
          'nevə ˋkɛəd fə ˌbrɔːdstɛəz sins ˌðen‖ ðə ˇweðə| wəz ə 'pein in ðə ˋnek‖
          it 'reind ən ˋreind| ən ðɛə wəz 'nouwɛə tə get əˋwei frəm it| ik,sept
          ðæt 'terəb| ould ˈʃeltə ˌðɛə‖
ˋmeivis   iz 'ðæt ˌmɛəri ɔn ðə ·left ·ðɛə‖
ˈʃɛərən   ˋjes| ənd ʃiːz ˋwɛəriŋ ə ˇdres| ai 'meid həː 'speʃli fə ðiː əˋkeiʒn̩‖
          bət it ˋfeidid| biˈkɔz əv ðə ˋrein| ənd ʃiːd 'nevə ˋwɛər it ə,gen‖
ˋmeivis   ai ˋskɛəsli ˋrekəgnaizd həː‖ 'wɔzn̩t həː 'hɛə ˋfɛə ˌðen‖ 'wɔt
          ˋeidʒ ˌwɔʒ ʃiː‖
ˈʃɛərən   'bɛəli ˋeit ai ʃəd ˌsei‖ həː 'hɛə 'steid ˇfɛə| til ʃiː wəz i'levn̩ ɔː
          ˋtwelv‖ 'ðen it 'tʃeindʒd tuː its ˋpreznt ˌʃeid‖ it wəz ə 'greit ˈʃeim|
          ʃiː ˋheitid it ˌtʃeindʒiŋ ˌðen| bət ʃiː əkˈseptid it 'veri ˋwel ˌleitə‖
          ən təˇdei| ʃiː 'kudn̩t kɛə ˋles‖
ˋmeivis   'didn̩t juː 'teik 'dʒein ən ˌsɛərə tə ·brɔːdstɛəz‖
ˈʃɛərən   ˋnou| 'ðei wə 'steiiŋ wið 'reiz ˋpɛərənts| ət ˋfɛəheivn̩‖ ðei
          inˋvɛəriəbli went ˌðɛər in ðə ˌsʌmə| bət 'mɛəri wəz ˋstreindʒ‖ ˋʃiː
          kud 'nevə ˋbɛə tə 'stei ˋeniwɛər ə,wei frəm ˌrei ən ˌmiː| wɛəræz
          ˋsɛərə ən ˇdʒein| wər ə ˋveri ˌdɛəriŋ ˌpɛə| frəm ðɛər ˋɔːliːis ˌdeiz‖
          'mɛəri 'nevə hæd ðə 'seim 'sens əv ədˋventʃə‖ ʃiːz ˋstil ˌfɛəli ˌwɛəri əv
          ˌfreʃ ˌfeisiz ən ˌpleisiz‖
ˋmeivis   ai 'dɛə sei ʃiːl ˋget 'les 'skɛəd ˋprezn̩tli‖
ˈʃɛərən   ʃiːl 'nevə kəm'pɛə wið 'dʒein ən ˋsɛərə fə ˌmeikiŋ ˌfrendz‖
ˋmeivis   bət ˋðɛər| it 'wudn̩t bi 'fɛə tuː ikˋspekt it‖ 'biːiŋ ˇtwinz| ðeiv
          ˈʃɛəd ˋevriθiŋ| ən ˋskɛəsli biːn ˋsepəreitid‖ wɛəræz 'mɛəriz biːn 'left
          tuː əːˋself tuː ə ˌgreit ikˌstent‖
ˈʃɛərən   ˋou| ðeiv ˋɔːlweiz biːn pri'pɛəd tə 'teik ˇmɛəri| wɛərˈevə ðei
          ˋwent‖ bət ˋʃi: 'dʒenrəli priˇfəːz| tə 'stei wið əːr 'eidʒid ˋpɛərənts‖
ˋmeivis   ʃiːl 'tɛər əːˋself əˋwei ˋwʌn ˌdei| juː ˌeidʒid ˌpɛərənt‖

Examples	shade	shed	shared	phase	fez	fares
	Bailey	belly	barely	cane	ken	cairn
	bane	Ben	bairn	spade	sped	spared

Mavis and Sharon

Mavis Where was this photograph taken?

Sharon It was taken at Broadstairs when we went there for a day. I've never cared for Broadstairs since then; the weather was a pain in the neck; it rained and rained and there was nowhere to get away from it except that terrible old shelter there.

Mavis Is that Mary on the left there?

Sharon Yes, and she's wearing a dress I made her specially for the occasion, but it faded because of the rain and she'd never wear it again.

Mavis I scarcely recognised her. Wasn't her hair fair then! What age was she?

Sharon Barely eight, I should say. Her hair stayed fair till she was eleven or twelve. Then it changed to its present shade. It was a great shame. She hated it changing then but she accepted it very well later, and today she couldn't care less.

Mavis Didn't you take Jane and Sarah to Broadstairs?

Sharon No, they were staying with Ray's parents at Fairhaven. They invariably went there in the summer, but Mary was strange, she could never bear to stay anywhere away from Ray and me, whereas Sarah and Jane were a very daring pair from their earliest days. Mary never had the same sense of adventure. She's still fairly wary of fresh faces and places.

Mavis I daresay she'll get less scared presently.

Sharon She'll never compare with Jane and Sarah for making friends.

Mavis But there, it wouldn't be fair to expect it; being twins, they've shared everything and scarcely been separated, whereas Mary's been left to herself to a great extent.

Sharon Oh, they've always been prepared to take Mary wherever they went, but she generally prefers to stay with her aged parents.

Mavis She'll tear herself away one day, you aged parent.

ˈnouəl ən ˈbraiən

ˈnouəl   ˈhauz jɔː ˈgaːdn̩ gouiŋ ˌnauədeiz ˌbraiən‖

ˈbraiən   ˈou‖ its ə ˈraiət əv ˌflauəz‖ inˈtaiəli ˈouiŋ tuː ˈaiəris əv ˌkɔːs‖

ˈnouəl   ˈaiəris jɔː ˌwaif‖ ɔːr ˈaiəris ðə ˈflauə‖

ˈbraiən   ˈou‖ ˈaiəris mai ˈwaif‖ ʃiː hæz ˈpauəf‖ inˈθjuːziæzm̩z‖ əz juː ˈmei
    ɔːlˈredi biː əˈwɛə‖ ən ʃiː ˈfainz ˈgrouiŋ ˇflauəz‖ ˈriəli inˈspaiəriŋ‖
    hauˈevə‖ ˈbiːiŋ ˈaiəris bai ˇneim‖ ʃiːz ˈɔːlwiz ədˈmaiəd ˌaiərisiz‖ ðə
    ˌflauəz‖ sou ʃiːz inˈdʒɔiiŋ əz ˈmeni vəˈraiətiz əz ʃiː ˈkæn‖ ʃiː ˈskauəz
    ðiː inˈtaiər ˈɛəriə‖ ˌtraiiŋ tə ˌfaind ˌnjuː wʌnz‖ bət wiː ˈɔːlsou inˈdʒɔi
    auə ˈvaiələts‖ ən ˈpiəniz‖ ənd auə ˈleidiz ˈdauəri‖ ənd . . .

ˈnouəl   auə ˈleidiz ˌdauəri‖ ˈhau əˈtræktiv‖

ˈbraiən   ˈjes‖ its ðiː aːˈkeiik ˌneim‖ fə ðə ˈgreip ˈhaiəsinθ‖ bət ˈhauz ˈjɔː
    ˌgaːdn̩‖ ˈɔːl əˈblouiŋ ən əˌgrouiŋ‖

ˈnouəl   ˈou‖ wiː hæd ə ˈfiəf‖ ikˌspiəriəns ə ˌdei ɔː tuː əˌgou‖ juː ˈnou
    ˈhauəd ˌseiəz‖

ˈbraiən   əv ˈseiəz ən ˌkauən‖ ðə ˌlɔiəz‖

ˈnouəl   ˈjes‖ wel ˈhauədz biːn ˈtʃɛəmən əv auə ˈpet səˌsaiəti‖ fə ˈjiəz‖
    ə ˈdʒenjuin ˈtauər əv ˈstreŋθ‖ ənd hiːz riˈtaiəriŋ‖ sou fiˈounə ˈhæd
    ðiː aiˇdiə‖ əv ˈpeiiŋ auə riˇspekts tuː im‖ bai ˈɔːgənaiziŋ ə ˈkwaiət lit‖
    riˈtaiəmənt ˌpaːti‖ in ˈauə ˈgaːdn̩‖

ˈbraiən   ˈhau ouvəˈpauəriŋ‖

ˈnouəl   ˈsou it trænˈspaiəd‖ auə miˈsteik ˌwɔz‖ tuː inˈvait ðə ˈpets‖ əz
    ˈwel əz ðə ˈpiːp‖‖ ai ˈɔːt tuː əv ˇriəlaizd‖ ˇðət ˈðæt ˈwɔzn̩t inˈtaiəli
    diˈzaiərəbl‖ ən ˈsou ɔːt fiˈounə‖ bət auər inˇθjuːziæzm̩‖ ˈouvəˈkeim
    auə ˈdʒʌdʒmənt‖

ˈbraiən   ai iˈmædʒən it wəz ˈkwait ə ˈraiətəs əˌfɛə‖

ˈnouəl   ˇraiətəs‖ it wəz ˈkeiɔs‖ aiv ˈrɛəli ikˈspiəriənst ˈeniθiŋ sou ˈɔːf‖‖
    it ˈstaːtid ˌkwaiətli iˌnʌf‖ bət wen ˈhauədz ˈsaiəmiːz ˇkæt‖ ˌstaːtid
    ˈklɔːiŋ ˈzoui ˈgauəz ˈaiəriʃ ˇteriə‖ ˈpændəˈmouniəm ˌbrouk ˌaut‖
    ˈænimz ˈflaiiŋ əˈbaut ˈevriwɛə‖ wið ðɛər aiəˈreit ˈounəz ˈtraiiŋ tə
    ˈkætʃ ðəm‖ it ˈsiːmd tə biː ˈauəz‖ biˌfɔː ðei ˌɔːl ˌkaːmd ˌdaun‖

ˈbraiən   ˈwɔt ə fiˈæskou‖ ənd hau ikˈstriːmli ˈtraiiŋ fə juː ˌɔːl‖ ai ikˈspekt
    ðə ˇgaːdn̩z‖ ʃouiŋ ˈsainz əv ˈvaiələns‖

ˈnouəl   its ˈruind‖ fiˈounəz in diˈspɛə‖ ˈhaːdli ə ˈflauə ˈleft‖ ənd its ðə
    ˈflauə ˌʃou in ˌtuː ɔː ˌθriː ˌwiːks‖

ˈbraiən   ou aim ˈʃuər ˈaiəris wil biː ˌeib‖ tə ˌhelp‖ aim ˈgouiŋ ˈhoum ˌnau‖
    sou ail ˈget əː tə ˈgiv fiˈounər ə ˈriŋ‖

ˈnouəl   ˈθæŋks ˈɔːfli ˌbraiən‖

Noel and Brian

Noel How's your garden going nowadays, Brian?

Brian Oh, it's a riot of flowers. Entirely owing to Iris, of course.

Noel Iris your wife, or iris the flower?

Brian Oh, Iris my wife. She has powerful enthusiasms, as you may already be aware, and she finds growing flowers really inspiring. However, being Iris by name she's always admired irises, the flowers, so she's enjoying as many varieties as she can. She scours the entire area trying to find new ones, but we also enjoy our violets and peonies and Our Lady's Dowry and . . .

Noel Our Lady's Dowry? How attractive!

Brian Yes, it's the archaic name for the grape hyacinth. But how's your garden? All a-blowing and a-growing?

Noel Oh, we had a fearful experience a day or two ago. You know Howard Sayers?

Brian Of Sayers and Cowan, the lawyers?

Noel Yes. Well, Howard's been chairman of our Pet Society for years, a genuine tower of strength, and he's retiring. So Fiona had the idea of paying our respects to him by organising a quiet little retirement party in our garden.

Brian How overpowering!

Noel So it transpired. Our mistake was to invite the pets as well as the people. I ought to have realised that that wasn't entirely desirable, and so ought Fiona, but our enthusiasm overcame our judgment.

Brian I imagine it was quite a riotous affair.

Noel Riotous? It was chaos! I've rarely experienced anything so awful. It started quietly enough, but when Howard's Siamese cat started clawing Zoe Gower's Irish terrier, pandemonium broke out. Animals flying about everywhere, with their irate owners trying to catch them. It seemed to be hours before they all calmed down.

Brian What a fiasco, and how extremely trying for you all. I expect the garden's showing signs of violence?

Noel It's ruined. Fiona's in despair! Hardly a flower left! And it's the Flower Show in two or three weeks.

Brian Oh, I'm sure Iris will be able to help. I'm going home now, so I'll get her to give Fiona a ring.

Noel Thanks awfully, Brian.

vә'rɔnikә әnd 'æntәni

vә'rɔnikә dә'ju: 'fi:l ‚strɔŋ‖

'æntәni 'kwait ‚strɔŋ‖ 'wai‖

vә'rɔnikә 'lets 'teik 'ðæt 'ould 'tʃɛә ‚daun‚stɛәz‖

'æntәni 'ou 'lɔ:d‖ 'nɔt 'streit 'ɑ:ftә ˇbrekfәst‖ 'li:vit fә'hɑ:f әn'auә| ‚kæn
ju:‖ it|bi'rɑ:ðәr ә'nɑ:sti 'dʒɔb‖

vә'rɔnikә 'ɔ:l ‚rait‖ 'ju: kәn'du: ðә'wɔʃiŋ ‚ʌp| әn'ail 'meik ðә‚bedz|
әn'ðen wi:l'si: hauju:'fi:l‖

'æntәni 'wai dәju:'wɔnt ðә'tʃɛә ri'mu:vd tә'dei‖ ðә‚mæn ‚wount
kә‚lektit ɔn‚sʌndi‖

vә'rɔnikә 'nou| ai'nou‖ hi:z'kʌmiŋ tә'pikit 'ʌp tә'mɔrou| bәt'ju: 'wount
biәt'houm ‚ðen| 'wilju:‖ әndaid'rɑ:ðә 'mu:vit 'daun wið'ju:
ðәnwið‚him‖ ju:'nou hau'kɛәlәs ðeikәn‚bi:‖

'æntәni 'ðæts ‚tru:‖ 'ou ‚wel| wi:'meiәz 'wel 'du:it 'nau ai‚spouz‖
ðә'wɔʃiŋ 'ʌp әnðә'bedz kәn'weit‖ 'wɛә wәju:'θiŋkiŋ әv'putiŋit‖

vә'rɔnikә ai'hædn̩t 'θɔ:t ә‚baut ‚ðæt‖ 'wɛә dju:'θiŋk‖

'æntәni it|bi'rɑ:ðәr ә'nju:sn̩s in‚hiә‖ 'kudwi: 'getit intәði:'ʌðә ‚ru:m‖

vә'rɔnikә wi:'mait ai‚spouz| bәtaiwәzin'tendiŋ tә'stɑ:t ɔnðә'nju: 'kә:tn̩z
ðis‚ɑ:f tә‚nu:n| әnaimә'freid ðәˇtʃɛә| wud'getin ðә'wei‖.

'æntәni 'kudn̩tju: 'du:ðәm in‚hiә‖

vә'rɔnikә aiˇkud| bәtits'i:ziә wiððә'big 'teib|‖

'æntәni 'jes| aii'mædʒәn it'iz‖ wel'luk| ifwi:'mu:v ðә'teib| in'hiә|
әn'teik ðәsi'ti: inˇðɛә| wi:kud'put ði:'ould ‚tʃɛәr| 'inðɛә 'wiðit|
әnju:dhæv'ru:m tә'wә:k ɔnðә'kә:tn̩z in'hiә‖

vә'rɔnikә 'wount 'ðæt bi:ә'nju:sn̩s fә‚ju:‖

'æntәni ai'ʃɑ:nt bi'hiә ‚mʌtʃ‖ ai'θɔ:t әvgouiŋ'ʌp tәðә'hɔspit|‖ tә'vizit
'ritʃәd 'beniŋ‖ hiz'waif 'kɑ:nt 'gou‖ ʃi:z'hæd tәgou'daun tә'wintʃәstә|
tәluk'ɑ:ftә hә:'mʌðә frә‚kʌp| әv‚deiz‖ ʃi:z'nɔt 'wel‖ hә:'mʌðәr
ai‚mi:n| souai'sed 'aid ‚gou‖

vә'rɔnikә 'ou| welin'ðæt ‚keis| wi:kud'mu:v ðә'teib| in'hiә‖ nau'wɔt
ʃәlwi:'mu:v 'fә:st‖

Veronica and Anthony

Veronica Do you feel strong?

Anthony Quite strong. Why?

Veronica Let's take that old chair downstairs.

Anthony Oh lord. Not straight after breakfast. Leave it for half an hour, can you? It'll be rather a nasty job.

Veronica All right. You can do the washing up and I'll make the beds, and then we'll see how you feel.

Anthony Why do you want the chair removed today? The man won't collect it on Sunday.

Veronica No, I know, he's coming to pick it up tomorrow, but you won't be at home then, will you? And I'd rather move it down with you than with him. You know how careless they can be.

Anthony That's true. Oh well, we may as well do it now, I suppose. The washing up and the beds can wait. Where were you thinking of putting it?

Veronica I hadn't thought about that. Where do you think?

Anthony It'll be rather a nuisance in here. Could we get it into the other room?

Veronica We might, I suppose, but I was intending to start on the new curtains this afternoon, and I'm afraid the chair would get in the way.

Anthony Couldn't you do them in here?

Veronica I could, but it's easier with the big table.

Anthony Yes, I imagine it is. Well, look, if we move the table in here, and take the settee in there, we could put the old chair in there with it, and you'd have room to work on the curtains in here.

Veronica Won't that be a nuisance for you?

Anthony I shan't be here much. I thought of going up to the hospital to visit Richard Benning. His wife can't go, she's had to go down to Winchester to look after her mother for a couple of days. She's not well. Her mother, I mean. So I said I'd go.

Veronica Oh, well in that case, we could move the table in here. Now what shall we move first?

'æntəni ənd ˈritʃəd

ˈritʃəd hʌˌlou ·æntəni‖ itˈiz ˌkaindəvjuː təˌkʌm‖ 'væləri ˈtouldmiː
 juːdˌsed juːˌwud| ʃiːwəzˈrɑːðər ʌpˈset ʃiːˈkudn̩t ˈkʌm həːˈself‖

ˈæntəni itsˈbæd ˈlʌkɔnəː| ðətəːˈmʌðə ʃudbiːˈil wailˈjɔːr inˌhɔspit|‖
bətˈhauəjuː ˈfiːliŋ‖ aiˈmʌssei juːˈluk ˌriːznəbli ˌwel‖

ˈritʃəd ˈou| ˈnɔt ˈtuː ˈbæd əˈtɔːl‖ aifeltˈpriti ˈrɔtn̩ iˈmiːdjətli ˈɑːftə
ðiːˌɔpə ˌreiʃn̩‖ bətaivˈgɔtɔn ˈveri ˈwel sinsˌðen‖ ðɛəˈkwait
ˈpliːzdwiðmiː‖

ˈæntəni ˈwilðei ˈletjuː ˌaut ·suːn djuːˈθiŋk‖

ˈritʃəd aiˈkiːp ˈɑːskiŋðəm ˌðæt| bətjuːˈnou hauðeiˈɑː| ðeiˈwount ˈprɔmis
ˌeniθiŋ‖ bətðəˈsəːdʒənz ˌdjuː təˌsiːmiː ɔnˌwenzdi‖ əndaiˈverimʌtʃ
ˈhoup ðətiːlˈtelmiː ˈðen| ˈwen aikənˈliːv‖ ˈpræps ˈnekst wiːkˈend‖

ˈæntəni juːˈmʌst əvmeidəˈgud riˈkʌvəri‖ əˈstʌmək ɔpəˌreiʃn̩| izˈnou
ˈlait ˈmætər əzəˌruːl‖

ˈritʃəd aiˈθiŋk aiˈmʌstəvbiːn ˈlʌki‖ ðɛəˈwəːnteni ˈkɔmpli ˈkeiʃn̩z
əˌpærəntli‖ souˈevriθiŋz biːnˈstreit ˈfɔːwəd‖

ˈæntəni ˈdʒɔli ˈgud‖ itˈmʌst əvbiːnəˈstrein ɔnjɔːˈwaif ˌðou‖

ˈritʃəd aimˈʃuər itˌhæz‖ ɔːlðouʃiːzbiːnˈveri ˈtʃiəf| wenʃiːzˈvizitid ˈmiː‖
bətitˈkɑːnt əvbiːnˌiːzi‖ əndiˈspeʃli wenʃiːˈhəːd ðətəːˈmʌðə wəzˌil‖

ˈæntəni ˈdʌz ðiːoulˈleidi ˈliv ɔnəːrˌoun‖

ˈritʃəd ˈjes| ʃiːˈdʌz‖ itsəˈbit əvəˈwʌri fərˌʌs| ˈeniwei‖ bətˈdʒenrəli|
ʃiːzˈveri ˈfit| souaiˈhoup itˈwount biːˈeniθiŋ ˈsiəriəs‖

ˈæntəni aiˈhoup ˈnɔt‖ ˈeni aiˈdiə ˈwen juːˈmait biːˈeib| təgetˈbæk
təˌwəːk‖

ˈritʃəd ˈif ðeiˈlet miːˈaut ˈnekst wiːkˈend‖ witʃaiˈhoup ðeiˈwil‖ aiˈθiŋk
aiˈʃud biˈbæk inəˈkʌp| əvˈwiːks‖ðeiˈsed aiˈɔːtn̩t təgouˈbæk ˈtuː ˈsuːn‖

ˈæntəni ˈhevn̩z ˌnou‖ ˈðæt wudbiriˈdikjələs‖ juːˈmʌsn̩t kʌmˈbæk|
tiljɔːˈriəli ˈfit əˌgen‖ nauˈdount fəˈget‖

Anthony and Richard

Richard Hello, Anthony. It is kind of you to come. Valerie told me you'd said you would. She was rather upset she couldn't come herself.

Anthony It's bad luck on her that her mother should be ill while you're in hospital. But how are you feeling? I must say you look reasonably well.

Richard Oh, not too bad at all. I felt pretty rotten immediately after the operation, but I've got on very well since then. They're quite pleased with me.

Anthony Will they let you out soon, do you think?

Richard I keep asking them that, but you know how they are. They won't promise anything. But the surgeon's due to see me on Wednesday and I very much hope that he'll tell me then when I can leave. Perhaps next weekend.

Anthony You must have made a good recovery. A stomach operation is no light matter, as a rule.

Richard I think I must have been lucky. There weren't any complications, apparently, so everything's been straightforward.

Anthony Jolly good. It must have been a strain on your wife, though.

Richard I'm sure it has, although she's been very cheerful when she's visited me. But it can't have been easy, and especially when she heard that her mother was ill.

Anthony Does the old lady live on her own?

Richard Yes, she does. It's a bit of a worry for us anyway. But generally she's very fit, so I hope it won't be anything serious.

Anthony I hope not. Any idea when you might be able to get back to work?

Richard If they let me out next weekend, which I hope they will, I think I should be back in a couple of weeks. They said I oughtn't to go back too soon.

Anthony Heavens, no. That would be ridiculous. You mustn't come back till you're really fit again. Now don't forget.